# Dealing with Data

## Data Analysis and Probability

BRITANNICA
**Mathematics in Context**

D1405284

**TEACHER'S GUIDE**

**HOLT, RINEHART** AND **WINSTON**

*Mathematics in Context* is a comprehensive curriculum for the middle grades.
It was developed in 1991 through 1997 in collaboration with the Wisconsin Center
for Education Research, School of Education, University of Wisconsin-Madison and
the Freudenthal Institute at the University of Utrecht, The Netherlands, with the
support of the National Science Foundation Grant No. 9054928.

The revision of the curriculum was carried out in 2003 through 2005, with the
support of the National Science Foundation Grant No. ESI 0137414.

## National Science Foundation

Opinions expressed are those of the authors
and not necessarily those of the Foundation.

de Jong, J. A.; Wijers, M.; Bakker, A.; Middleton, J. A.; Simon, A. N.; and Burrill, G.
(2006). *Dealing with data.* In Wisconsin Center for Education Research &
Freudenthal Institute (Eds.), *Mathematics in context.* Chicago: Encyclopædia
Britannica, Inc.

The Teacher's Guide for this unit was prepared by David C. Webb, Beth R. Cole,
Monica Wijers, Dédé de Haan, and Sonia Palha.

ISBN 0-03-039827-4

2 3 4 5 6   073   09 08 07 06

# The *Mathematics in Context* Development Team

## Development 1991–1997

The initial version of *Dealing with Data* was developed by Jan Auke de Jong and Monica Wijers.
It was adapted for use in American schools by James A. Middleton, Aaron N. Simon, and Gail Burrill.

### Wisconsin Center for Education Research Staff

Thomas A. Romberg
*Director*

Joan Daniels Pedro
*Assistant to the Director*

Gail Burrill
*Coordinator*

Margaret R. Meyer
*Coordinator*

### Freudenthal Institute Staff

Jan de Lange
*Director*

Els Feijs
*Coordinator*

Martin van Reeuwijk
*Coordinator*

### Project Staff

Jonathan Brendefur
Laura Brinker
James Browne
Jack Burrill
Rose Byrd
Peter Christiansen
Barbara Clarke
Doug Clarke
Beth R. Cole
Fae Dremock
Mary Ann Fix

Sherian Foster
James A, Middleton
Jasmina Milinkovic
Margaret A. Pligge
Mary C. Shafer
Julia A. Shew
Aaron N. Simon
Marvin Smith
Stephanie Z. Smith
Mary S. Spence

Mieke Abels
Nina Boswinkel
Frans van Galen
Koeno Gravemeijer
Marja van den Heuvel-Panhuizen
Jan Auke de Jong
Vincent Jonker
Ronald Keijzer
Martin Kindt

Jansie Niehaus
Nanda Querelle
Anton Roodhardt
Leen Streefland
Adri Treffers
Monica Wijers
Astrid de Wild

## Revision 2003–2005

The revised version of *Dealing with Data* was developed by Arthur Bakker and Monica Wijers.
It was adapted for use in American schools by Gail Burrill.

### Wisconsin Center for Education Research Staff

Thomas A. Romberg
*Director*

David C. Webb
*Coordinator*

Gail Burrill
*Editorial Coordinator*

Margaret A. Pligge
*Editorial Coordinator*

### Freudenthal Institute Staff

Jan de Lange
*Director*

Truus Dekker
*Coordinator*

Mieke Abels
*Content Coordinator*

Monica Wijers
*Content Coordinator*

### Project Staff

Sarah Ailts
Beth R. Cole
Erin Hazlett
Teri Hedges
Karen Hoiberg
Carrie Johnson
Jean Krusi
Elaine McGrath

Margaret R. Meyer
Anne Park
Bryna Rappaport
Kathleen A. Steele
Ana C. Stephens
Candace Ulmer
Jill Vettrus

Arthur Bakker
Peter Boon
Els Feijs
Dédé de Haan
Martin Kindt

Nathalie Kuijpers
Huub Nilwik
Sonia Palha
Nanda Querelle
Martin van Reeuwijk

**Cover photo credits: (left)** © Creatas; **(middle, right)** © Getty Images

**Illustrations**
**x (bottom)** Jason Millet; **xviii** Christine McCabe/ © Encyclopædia Britannica, Inc.; **1, 3, 5, 26,** Holly Cooper-Olds; **34–38** © Encyclopædia Britannica, Inc.; **43 (top)** Holly Cooper-Olds

**Photographs**
**x** Amos Morgan/PhotoDisc/Getty Images; **xvii** PhotoDisc/Getty Images; **xviii** Victoria Smith/HRW; **4** © Corbis; **8** © Kim Steele/Getty Images/PhotoDisc; **9** © Getty Images/Digital Vision; **12 (all)** Library of Congress, Washington D.C.; **13** John Adams, Courtesy of the National Collection of Fine Arts, Smithsonian Institution, Washington D.C.; Thomas Jefferson, Courtesy of the White House Collection, Washington, D.C.; James Monroe, Courtesy of the Independence National Historical Park Collection, Philadelphia; Martin Van Buren, Courtesy of Chicago Historical Society; Woodrow Wilson, © Encyclopædia Britannica, Inc.; **(all others)** Library of Congress, Washington, D.C.; **14** Calvin Coolidge, Herbert C. Hoover © Encyclopædia Britannica, Inc.; Franklin D. Roosevelt, UPI; Harry S. Truman, Courtesy of the U.S. Signal Corps; Dwight D. Eisenhower, Fabian Bachrach; Lyndon B. Johnson, Courtesy of the National Archives, Washington, D.C.; Gerald R. Ford, AP/Wide World Photos; James E. Carter, The Carter Center/Billy Howard; Ronald Reagan, Courtesy Ronald Reagan Library; George Bush, William J. Clinton, White House photo/Library of Congress, Washington, D.C.; George W. Bush, Eric Draper/White House photo; **(all other presidents)** Library of Congress, Washington, D.C.; **(bottom)** PhotoDisc/Getty Images; **16** Courtesy of the U.S. Signal Corps; **17** Victoria Smith/HRW; **18** © Corbis; **21** Edward R. Tufte, The Visual Display of Quantitative Information, 2nd Edition, Graphics Press LLC, 2001; **25** Bassano and Vandyk, Elliott and Fry; **28** Victoria Smith/HRW; **29** © Larry Brownstein/Getty Images/PhotoDisc; **30** © PhotoDisc/Getty Images; **31** © Brooks Kraft/Corbis; **34** Photo by Richard D. Huseth http://users.ev1.net/~rhuseth/; **39 (top)** © Comstock, Inc., © Corel, PhotoDisc/Getty Images; **(bottom)** © Corbis; **40 (top)** © Corbis; **(bottom)** © Comstock, Inc.; **41 (top)** © ImageState; **(bottom)** © Corbis

# Contents

## Dear Teacher,

Welcome! *Mathematics in Context* is designed to reflect the National Council of Teachers of Mathematics *Principles and Standards for School Mathematics* and the results of decades of classroom-based education research. *Mathematics in Context* was designed according to principles of Realistic Mathematics Education, a Dutch approach to mathematics teaching and learning where mathematical content is grounded in a variety of realistic contexts to promote student engagement and understanding of mathematics. The term *realistic* is meant to convey that the contexts and mathematics can be made "real in your mind." Rather than relying on you to explain and demonstrate generalized definitions, rules, or algorithms, students investigate questions directly related to a particular context and develop mathematical understanding and meaning from that context.

The curriculum encompasses nine units per grade level. This unit is designed to be the third in the Data Analysis and Probability strand, but it also lends itself to independent use—to introduce students to experiences that will enrich their understanding and use of statistical measures and graphs.

In addition to the Teacher's Guide and Student Books, *Mathematics in Context* offers the following components that will inform and support your teaching:

- *Teacher Implementation Guide,* which provides an overview of the complete system and resources for program implementation.

- *Number Tools* and *Algebra Tools,* which are blackline master resources that serve as review sheets or practice pages to support the development of basic skills and extend student understanding of concepts developed in Number and Algebra units.

- *Mathematics in Context Online,* which is a rich, balanced resource for teachers, students, and parents looking for additional information, activities, tools, and support to further students' mathematical understanding and achievements.

Thank you for choosing *Mathematics in Context.* We wish you success and inspiration!

Sincerely,

*The Mathematics in Context Development Team*

# *Dealing with Data* and the NCTM Principles and Standards for School Mathematics for Grades 6-8

The process standards of Problem Solving, Reasoning and Proof, Communication, Connections, and Representation are addressed across all *Mathematics in Context* units.

In addition, this unit specifically addresses the following PSSM content standards and expectations:

## Data Analysis and Probability

In grades 6–8 all students should:

- formulate questions and collect data about a characteristic shared by two populations or different characteristics within one population;

- select, create, and use appropriate graphical representations of data, including histograms, box plots, and scatterplots;

- find, use, and interpret measures of center and spread, including mean and interquartile range;

- discuss and understand the correspondence between data sets and their graphical representations, especially histograms, stem-and-leaf plots, box plots, and scatterplots; and

- use observations about differences between two or more samples to make conjectures about the populations from which the samples were taken.

# Math in the Unit

## Prior Knowledge

This unit assumes students can do the following with understanding:

- add and subtract whole and decimal numbers to the tenths place;
- multiply with two-digit whole numbers:
- divide a whole number into a whole or decimal number to the tenths place;
- use a number line (addressed earlier in *Picturing Numbers, Models You Can Count On,* and practiced in *Number Tools);*
- use a table to organize information; and
- make bar graphs (addressed earlier in *Picturing Numbers).*

In addition, it is helpful if students are familiar with percents and with plotting points on a coordinate axis. It is also helpful if students have been introduced to the compensation strategy of finding the mean from the unit *Picturing Numbers.*

| Litter | Number of Babies in Litter | | | | | | | | |
|---|---|---|---|---|---|---|---|---|---|
| | 1 | 2 | 3 | 4 | 5 | 6 | 7 | 8 | 9 |
| A | 🐭 | 🐭 | 🐭 | 🐭 | 🐭 | 🐭 | | | |
| B | 🐭 | 🐭 | 🐭 | 🐭 | 🐭 | 🐭 | 🐭 | ✕ | ✕ |
| C | 🐭 | 🐭 | 🐭 | 🐭 | 🐭 | 🐭 | 🐭 | ✕ | ✕ |
| D | 🐭 | 🐭 | 🐭 | 🐭 | 🐭 | 🐭 | | | |
| E | 🐭 | 🐭 | 🐭 | 🐭 | 🐭 | 🐭 | 🐭 | | |
| F | 🐭 | 🐭 | 🐭 | 🐭 | 🐭 | 🐭 | | | |
| G | 🐭 | 🐭 | 🐭 | 🐭 | 🐭 | 🐭 | 🐭 | ✕ | ✕ |
| H | 🐭 | 🐭 | 🐭 | 🐭 | 🐭 | 🐭 | 🐭 | ✕ | |
| I | 🐭 | 🐭 | 🐭 | 🐭 | 🐭 | | | | |
| J | 🐭 | 🐭 | 🐭 | 🐭 | 🐭 | | | | |
| K | 🐭 | 🐭 | 🐭 | 🐭 | 🐭 | 🐭 | ✕ | | |
| L | 🐭 | 🐭 | 🐭 | 🐭 | 🐭 | 🐭 | 🐭 | ✕ | ✕ |
| M | 🐭 | 🐭 | 🐭 | 🐭 | 🐭 | 🐭 | ✕ | | |
| N | 🐭 | 🐭 | 🐭 | 🐭 | 🐭 | | | | |
| O | 🐭 | 🐭 | 🐭 | 🐭 | 🐭 | 🐭 | 🐭 | ✕ | ✕ |
| P | 🐭 | 🐭 | 🐭 | 🐭 | 🐭 | | | | |
| Q | 🐭 | 🐭 | 🐭 | 🐭 | 🐭 | | | | |
| R | 🐭 | 🐭 | 🐭 | 🐭 | 🐭 | 🐭 | | | |

*Dealing with Data* is the third unit in the Data Analysis and Probability strand, following the units *Picturing Numbers* and *Take a Chance.* In this unit, students are introduced to different ways of organizing and interpreting large sets of data. They must, for example, organize and interpret data from a real historical data set on heights of 1,024 fathers and sons in order to decide whether they agree with the conclusion of the original researchers that, in general, sons grow to be taller than their fathers.

Students eventually identify a line that splits the scatter plot (that is, the line $y = x$), and use this line to draw conclusions about whether sons generally are taller than their fathers. They also consider such things as how to reorganize the list of data to make it more helpful and whether the sample was representative of the total population.

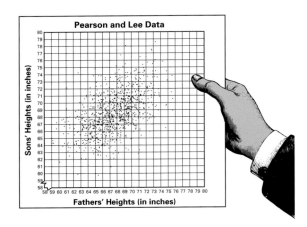

Using this and other sets of data, including data they collect themselves, students read graphs and interpret scatter plots, stem-and-leaf plots, dot plots on a number line, histograms, and box plots.

They study data collection methods and are introduced to the concept of *sample.* Students look for relationships among variables and study patterns in data sets. They calculate the mean, mode, and median and relate these measures of central tendency to graphs representing the same data. Students also consider the strengths and weaknesses of each measure of central tendency and of each type of graph.

When students have finished the unit they:

- can create and interpret different kinds of graphs: scatter plots, box plots, stem-and-leaf plots, histograms, and number line plots;
  - Students are introduced to these types of graphs in this unit. These graphs will also be revisited in the unit *Insights into Data.*
  - can collect data and represent them in tabular and graphic form;

- create their own diagrams as well as make stem-and-leaf plots, scatter plots, histograms, number line plots, and box plots;
- can identify advantages and disadvantages of different graphical representations;

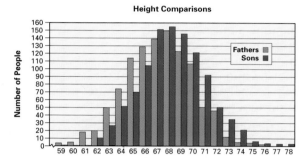

- describe data numerically using mean, median, mode, quartile, range, maximum, and minimum;
  - Students know different ways to find these descriptive statistics from a given data set.
  - Students are able to tell whether mean, mode, or median, together with measures of "spread," are useful for describing a given data set.
- understand the concepts of representative sample and population; and
  - These concepts are introduced here and are revisited and formalized in the units *Insights into Data* and *Great Predictions.*

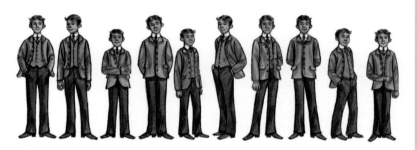

- use data, graphs, and numeric characteristics to build arguments and compare data sets.
  - Students can see patterns and other features of data sets in graphs and other diagrams.

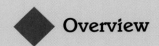
# The Data Analysis and Probability Strand: An Overview

One thing is for sure: our lives are full of uncertainty. We are not certain what the weather will be tomorrow or which team will win a game or how accurate a pulse rate really is. Data analysis and probability are ways to help us measure variability and uncertainty. A central feature of both data analysis and probability is that these disciplines help us make numerical conjectures about important questions.

The techniques and tools of data analysis and probability allow us to understand general patterns for a set of outcomes from a given situation such as tossing a coin, but it is important to remember that a given outcome is only part of the larger pattern. Many students initially tend to think of individual cases and events, but gradually they learn to think of all features of data sets and of probabilities as proportions in the long run.

## The MiC Approach to Data Analysis and Probability

The Data Analysis and Probability units in MiC emphasize dealing with data, developing an understanding of chance and probability, using probability in situations connected to data analysis, and developing critical thinking skills.

The strand begins with students' intuitive understanding of the data analysis concepts of *most*, *least*, and *middle* in relation to different types of *graphical representations* that show *the distribution of data* and the probability concepts of *fairness* and *chance*. As students gradually formalize these ideas, they use a variety of counting strategies and graphical representations. In the culminating units of this strand, they use formal rules and strategies for calculating probabilities and finding measures of central tendency and spread.

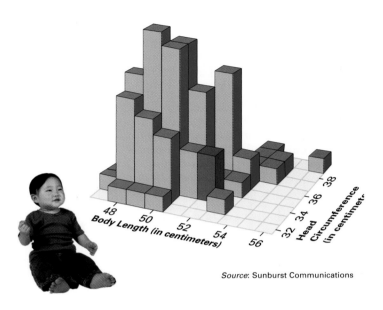

*Source*: Sunburst Communications

Throughout this development, there is a constant emphasis on interpreting conclusions made by students and suggested in the media or other sources. In order for students to make informed decisions, they must understand how information is collected, represented, and summarized, and they examine conjectures made from the information based on this understanding. They learn about all phases of an investigative cycle, starting with questions, collecting data, analyzing them, and communicating about the conclusions. They are introduced to inference-by-sampling to collect data and reflect on possible sources of bias. They develop notions of random sampling, variation and central tendency, correlation, and regression. Students create, interpret, and reflect on a wide range of graphical representations of data and relate these representations to numerical summaries such as mean, mode, and range.

## Organization of the Strand

Statistical reasoning based on data is addressed in all Data Analysis and Probability units. Students' work in these units is organized into two substrands: Data Analysis and Chance. As illustrated in the following map of the strand, the three core units that focus on data analysis are *Picturing Numbers*, *Dealing with Data*, and *Insights into Data*. The two units that focus on probability are *Take a Chance* and *Second Chance*. The sixth core unit in this strand, *Great Predictions*, integrates data analysis and probability.

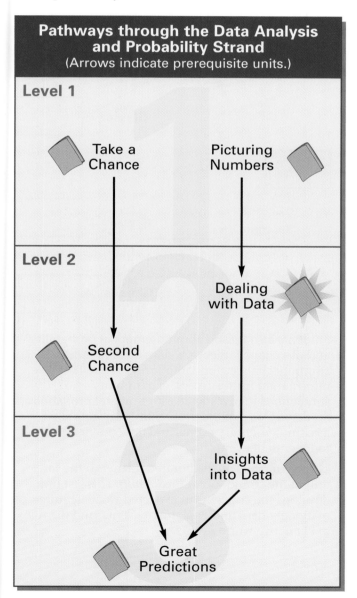

**Pathways through the Data Analysis and Probability Strand**
(Arrows indicate prerequisite units.)

Level 1

Take a Chance    Picturing Numbers

Level 2

Dealing with Data

Second Chance

Level 3

Insights into Data

Great Predictions

## Data Analysis

In the units of the Data Analysis substrand, students collect, depict, describe, and analyze data. Using the statistical tools they develop, they make inferences and draw conclusions based on data sets.

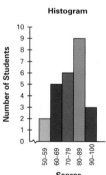

The substrand begins with *Picturing Numbers*. Students collect data and display them in tabular and graphical forms, such as histograms, number line plots, and pie charts. Measures of central tendency, such as the mean, are used informally as students interpret data and make conjectures.

In *Dealing with Data*, students create and interpret scatter plots, box plots, and stem-and-leaf plots, in addition to other graphical representations. The mean, median, mode, range, and quartiles are used to summarize data sets. Students investigate data sets with outliers and make conclusions about the appropriate use of the mean and median.

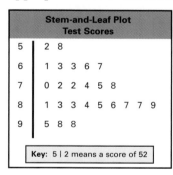

**Stem-and-Leaf Plot Test Scores**

| 5 | 2 8 |
| 6 | 1 3 3 6 7 |
| 7 | 0 2 2 4 5 8 |
| 8 | 1 3 3 4 5 6 7 7 9 |
| 9 | 5 8 8 |

Key: 5 | 2 means a score of 52

Sampling is addressed across this substrand, but in particular in *Insights into Data*, starting with informal notions of representative samples, randomness, and bias. Students gather data using various sampling techniques and investigate the differences between a survey and a sample. They create a simulation to answer questions about a situation. Students also consider how graphical information can be misleading, and they are introduced informally to the concepts of regression and correlation.

In *Great Predictions*, students learn to recognize the variability in random samples and deepen their understanding of the key statistical concepts of randomness, sample size, and bias. As the capstone unit to the Data Analysis and Probability strand, data and chance concepts and techniques are integrated and used to inform conclusions about data.

## Chance

Beginning with the concept of fairness, *Take a Chance* progresses to everyday situations involving chance. Students use coins and number cubes to conduct repeated trials of an experiment. A chance ladder is used as a model throughout the unit to represent the range from impossible to certain and to ground the measure of chance as a number between 0 and 1. Students also use tree diagrams to organize and count, and they use benchmark fractions, ratios, and percents to describe the probability of various outcomes and combinations.

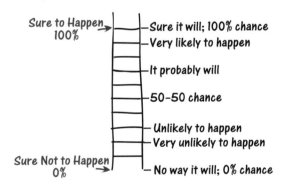

The second probability unit, *Second Chance,* further develops students' understanding of fairness and the quantification of chance. Students make chance statements from data presented in two-way tables and in graphs.

|  | Men | Women | Total |
|---|---|---|---|
| **Glasses** | 32 | 3 | 35 |
| **No Glasses** | 56 | 39 | 95 |
| **Total** | 88 | 42 | 130 |

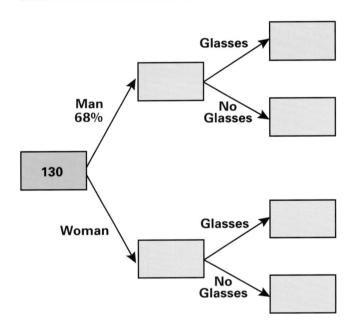

Students also reason about theoretical probability and use chance trees as well as an area model to compute chances for compound events. They use information from surveys, experiments, and simulations to investigate experimental probability. Students also explore probability concepts such as complementary events and dependent and independent events.

These concepts are elaborated further in the final unit of the strand, *Great Predictions.* This last unit develops the concepts of expected value, features of independent and dependent events, and the role of chance in world events.

## Critical Reasoning

Critical reasoning about data and chance is a theme that exists in every unit of the Data Analysis and Probability strand. In *Picturing Numbers*, students informally consider factors that influence data collection, such as the wording of questions on a survey, and they compare different graphs of the same data set. They also use statistical data to build arguments for or against environmental policies.

In *Take a Chance*, students use their informal knowledge of fairness and equal chances as they evaluate decision-making strategies.

In *Dealing with Data*, students explore how the graphical representation of a data set influences the conjectures and conclusions that are suggested by the data. They compare advantages and disadvantages of various graphs and explore what you learn from using different measures of central tendency.

Throughout the curriculum, students are asked to view representations critically. Developing a critical attitude is especially promoted in *Insights into Data*, when students analyze graphs from mass media.

In *Second Chance*, students explore the notion of dependency (for instance, the relation of gender and wearing glasses) and analyze statements about probabilities (for instance, about guessing during a test).

In *Great Predictions*, students study unusual samples to decide whether they occurred by chance or for some other reason (pollution, for instance). They explore how expected values and probability can help them make decisions and when this information could be misleading.

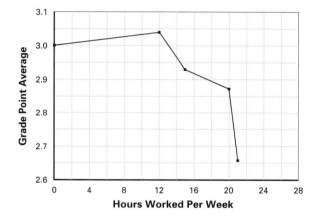

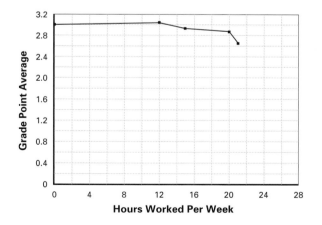

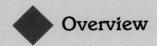

# Student Assessment in Mathematics in Context

As recommended by the NCTM *Principles and Standards for School Mathematics* and research on student learning, classroom assessment should be based on evidence drawn from several sources. An assessment plan for a *Mathematics in Context* unit may draw from the following overlapping sources:

- **observation—As students work individually or in groups, watch for evidence of their understanding of the mathematics.**

- **interactive responses—Listen closely to how students respond to your questions and to the responses of other students.**

- **products—Look for clarity and quality of thought in students' solutions to problems completed in class, homework, extensions, projects, quizzes, and tests.**

## Assessment Pyramid

When designing a comprehensive assessment program, the assessment tasks used should be distributed across the following three dimensions: mathematics content, levels of reasoning, and difficulty level. The Assessment Pyramid, based on Jan de Lange's theory of assessment, is a model used to suggest how items should be distributed across these three dimensions. Over time, assessment questions should "fill" the pyramid.

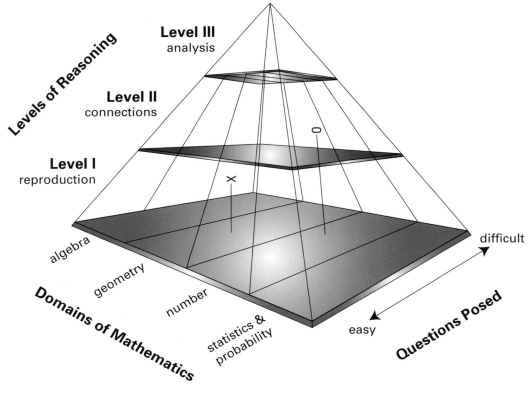

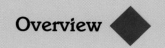

## Levels of Reasoning

### Level I questions typically address:

- recall of facts and definitions and
- use of technical skills, tools, and standard algorithms.

As shown in the pyramid, Level I questions are not necessarily easy. For example, Level I questions may involve complicated computation problems. In general, Level I questions assess basic knowledge and procedures that may have been emphasized during instruction. The format for this type of question is usually short answer, fill-in, or multiple choice. On a quiz or test, Level I questions closely resemble questions that are regularly found in a given unit substituted with different numbers and/or contexts.

### Level II questions require students to:

- integrate information;
- decide which mathematical models or tools to use for a given situation; and
- solve unfamiliar problems in a context, based on the mathematical content of the unit.

Level II questions are typically written to elicit short or extended responses. Students choose their own strategies, use a variety of mathematical models, and explain how they solved a problem.

### Level III questions require students to:

- make their own assumptions to solve open-ended problems;
- analyze, interpret, synthesize, reflect; and
- develop one's own strategies or mathematical models.

Level III questions are always open-ended problems. Often, more than one answer is possible, and there is a wide variation in reasoning and explanations. There are limitations to the type of Level III problems that students can be reasonably expected to respond to on time-restricted tests.

The instructional decisions a teacher makes as he or she progresses through a unit may influence the level of reasoning required to solve problems. If a method of problem solving required to solve a Level III problem is repeatedly emphasized during instruction, the level of reasoning required to solve a Level II or III problem may be reduced to recall knowledge, or Level I reasoning. A student who does not master a specific algorithm during a unit but solves a problem correctly using his or her own invented strategy may demonstrate higher-level reasoning than a student who memorizes and applies an algorithm.

The "volume" represented by each level of the Assessment Pyramid serves as a guideline for the distribution of problems and use of score points over the three reasoning levels.

These assessment design principles are used throughout *Mathematics in Context*. The Goals and Assessment charts that highlight ongoing assessment opportunities—on pages xvi and xvii of each Teacher's Guide—are organized according to levels of reasoning.

In the Lesson Notes section of the Teacher's Guide, ongoing assessment opportunities are also shown in the Assessment Pyramid icon located at the bottom of the Notes column.

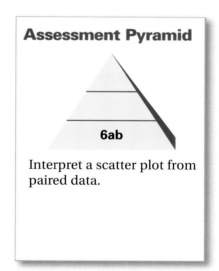

**Assessment Pyramid**

6ab

Interpret a scatter plot from paired data.

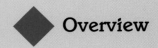
# Goals and Assessment

In the *Mathematics in Context* curriculum, unit goals, organized according to levels of reasoning described in the Assessment Pyramid on page xiv, relate to the strand goals and the NCTM *Principles and Standards for School Mathematics*. The *Mathematics in Context* curriculum is designed to help students demonstrate their understanding of mathematics in

each of the categories listed below. Ongoing assessment opportunities are also indicated on their respective pages throughout the Teacher's Guide by an Assessment Pyramid icon.

It is important to note that the attainment of goals in one category is not a prerequisite to attaining those in another category. In fact, students should progress simultaneously toward

several goals in different categories. The Goals and Assessment table is designed to support preparation of an assessment plan.

| | Goal | Ongoing Assessment Opportunities | Unit Assessment Opportunities |
|---|---|---|---|
| **Level I: Conceptual and Procedural Knowledge** | **1.** Create and interpret a stem-and-leaf plot, histogram, or box plot from a single data set. | **Section C** p. 20, #18<br>**Section D** p. 29, #8ab<br>**Section E** p. 43, #15abc | **Quiz 1** #1d<br>**Quiz 2** #2ab<br>**Test** #1bd, 2c, 3ab, 4ab<br>**Statistics Project** |
| | **2.** Create and interpret a scatter plot from paired data, and understand the meaning of the line $y = x$. | **Section B** p. 9, #6ab | **Quiz 1** #2abc |
| | **3.** Collect, organize, and interpret data in tabular form. | **Section A** p. 5, Activity<br>**Section C** p. 15, #8ab<br>p. 16, #9b<br>**Section D** p. 30, #10 | **Quiz 1** #1abc<br>**Quiz 2** #2a<br>**Statistics Project** |
| | **4.** Find and interpret the mean, median, mode, or range of a data set. | **Section D** p. 27, #8c<br>p. 28, #7a<br>**Section E** p. 40, #11c | **Quiz 2** #1abde<br>**Test** #1d, 2cf<br>**Statistics Project** |

| | Goal | Ongoing Assessment Opportunities | Unit Assessment Opportunities |
|---|---|---|---|
| **Level II: Reasoning, Communicating, Thinking, and Making Connections** | **5.** Understand the importance of a representative sample. | **Section A** p. 6, FFR | **Quiz 1** #1b, 2d<br>**Quiz 2** #1c<br>**Test** #4b |
| | **6.** Compare different representations and understand their differences and similarities. | **Section B** p. 11, #FFR<br>**Section C** p. 19, #16<br>p. 24, FFR | **Test** #2e<br>**Statistics Project** |

| | Goal | Ongoing Assessment Opportunities | Unit Assessment Opportunities |
|---|---|---|---|
| **Level III: Modeling, Generalizing, and Non-Routine Problem Solving** | **7.** Understand the need to organize and summarize a large set of data in order for it to be useful. | **Section A** p. 2, #4 | **Test** #1a |
| | **8.** Build an argument based on statistical measures and graphs. | **Section C** p. 20, #18<br>**Section E** p. 40, #11c | **Test** #1d, 2d<br>**Statistics Project** |
| | **9.** Develop a critical attitude toward using statistical methods to solve problems and make a decision. | **Section A** p. 3, #5c<br>**Section D** p. 29, #8d<br>p. 31, #12d | **Test** #2g<br>**Quiz 2** #1f |
| | **10.** Solve problems by choosing appropriate statistical measures and graphs. | **Section E** p. 40, #11abc | **Test** #1c, 2g<br>**Statistics Project** |

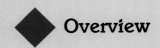
# Materials Preparation

The following items are the necessary materials and resources to be used by the teacher and students throughout the unit. For further details, see the Section Overviews and the Materials section at the top of the Hints and Comments column on each teacher page. Note: Some contexts and problems can be enhanced through the use of optional materials. These optional materials are listed in the corresponding Hints and Comments column.

## Student Resources

Quantities listed are per student.

- **Letter to the Family**
- **Student Activity Sheets 1–4**
- **Extra copy of Student Activity Sheets 3 and 4**

## Teacher Resources

Quantities listed are per class.

- **Transparency of data collected by students**

## Student Materials

Quantities listed are per pair of students, unless otherwise noted.

- **Calculator**
- **Colored pencils — red, green, and blue**
- **Copy of Appendix A**
- **Graph paper (3 sheets per student)**
- **Measuring tape**
- **Ruler or straightedge**
- **Scissors**
- **String (30 centimeters per student)**

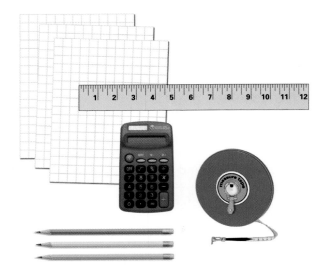

# Student Material and Teaching Notes

# ◆ Contents

**Presidents' Ages at Inauguration**

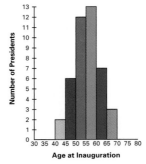

## Dear Student,

How big is your hand? Do you think it is bigger than, smaller than, or the same size as most people's hands? How can you find out?

How fast does a cheetah run? Do you think it runs much faster than, a little faster than, or at about the same speed as other animals? How can you find out?

Do tall people have tall children?

How can you find out?

In the *Mathematics in Context* unit *Dealing with Data*, you will examine questions like these and learn how to answer them. By collecting and examining data, you can answer questions that are interesting and often important.

While you are working through this unit, think of your own questions that you can answer by collecting and examining data. One of the best uses of mathematics is to help you answer questions you find interesting.

Sincerely,

*The Mathematics in Context Development Team*

## Section Focus

Students explore a large data set that compares the heights of fathers to the heights of their sons. This is a historical data set from around 1900, of Pearson and Lee, two scientists. This data set will be further explored and analyzed throughout the rest of the unit. Students understand the need to organize and summarize a large data set; they evaluate statements about the data; and they are introduced to the concept of sampling.

## Pacing and Planning

| Day 1: The Turn of the Century | | Student pages 1–5 |
|---|---|---|
| INTRODUCTION | Problem 1 | Introduce the context of collecting data on peoples' heights. |
| CLASSWORK | Problems 2–5 | Investigate a large data set that compares the heights of fathers with the heights of their sons. |
| HOMEWORK | Activity: Page 5 | Activity: Collect data on the heights of mothers and daughters. |

| Day 2: The Sample of Pearson and Lee | | Student pages 4–6 |
|---|---|---|
| INTRODUCTION | Problems 6 and 7 | Discuss how to get a fair sample from a large population. |
| CLASSWORK | Activity: Page 5 | Organize and discuss the mother-daughter data collected for homework. |
| HOMEWORK | Check Your Work and For Further Reflection | Student self-assessment: Sampling and organization of large data sets. |

Additional Resources: Additional Practice, Section A, Student Book page 46

## Materials

### Student Resources

Quantities listed are per student.

- Letter to the Family

### Teachers Resources

Quantities listed are per student.

- blank transparency (one of each per class);
- overhead projector

### Student Materials

No resource required

* See Hints and Comments for optional materials.

## Learning Lines

### Using Data

In this section, students begin to understand how data are used to answer questions. Students begin to think about what data is, where it comes from, and how it is used. Students evaluate various arguments based on the presented data about the heights of fathers and their sons to see whether sons are taller than their fathers. The data set explored in this section is a paired data set: each value in one data set (a father's height) is related to one value in the other data set (a son's height). This data set reappears throughout the unit.

### Sampling

Collecting data is the beginning of the process that renders statistics. In some cases, it is important to ensure that the data collected are representative of the population of interest. If the whole population cannot be studied, a sample can be taken. In this section, students are introduced to the idea of a representative sample. This is done in an informal way. The term *sample* is used, and a definition is given. The term *representative* is not used. Students reflect on the way a sample is chosen.

**Sampling**

By doing so they learn to understand that sampling should be done in a "proper way" in order to make valid conclusions possible. Students develop a critical attitude towards surveys and how data are collected, including the process of sampling. Sampling is revisited and formalized in the units *Insights into Data* and *Great Predictions*.

### Organizing and Representing Large Data Sets

If a data set is very large, organizing techniques must be used to make sense of the data in some way. The data set students study in Appendix A has too many entries for students to get an idea of trends or patterns in the data by just looking at the numbers.

Students think about ways to organize these data. In this section, students describe data in words (a qualitative description) or they use numbers.

> Tiwanda says, "I can say that the sons were generally taller than their fathers, because the total height of all of the fathers is 72,033 inches. The total height of all of the sons is 73,126 inches."

Numbers that summarize sets of data are called *statistics*; these are used to make sense of data. Graphs can also be used to make sense of data by giving a global visual picture of the data set. In this section, no graphs are used yet. In the rest of this unit, students will learn to use a variety of graphs and statistics to make sense of data.

### At the End of This Section: Learning Outcomes

Students will:

- understand the importance of a sample being chosen in a proper way;
- understand the need to organize and summarize a large set of data in order for it to be useful; and
- develop a critical attitude toward surveys and sampling.

## Notes

You can start this section with a short class discussion about the heights of people. Discuss whether or not students think that people have gotten taller over the last century. After the introduction, you may wish to have students begin working on problem 1 in small groups.

**1a** Students may argue that 18 is too young or too old depending on their own experiences of when people reach their adult height. Eighteen is a reasonable choice because *most* people are full height by 18.

**1b** Students should have a chance to think about this question, and then there should be a discussion so that students are convinced that this is a question worth investigating.

**A** 

# Are People Getting Taller?

## The Turn of the Century: The Pearson and Lee Investigation

"Have you ever slept in a really old bed and noticed it was a lot smaller than your bed?"

Other people have noticed this too. Around 1900, statisticians Karl Pearson and Alice Lee decided to collect data that would help them determine whether or not children grow to be taller than their parents. They asked people to measure the height of each member of their family over the age of 18.

1. **a.** Why did everyone have to be over 18 years old for the survey?

   **b. Reflect** Why do you think it might be important to see if children grow taller than their parents?

---

### Reaching All Learners

**Vocabulary Building**

You may want to discuss the term survey. A survey is a way of collecting data. The term *statistician* may be unfamiliar to students. Relating it to the word mathematician may help students understand that a statistician is a person who studies statistics.

## Solutions and Samples

1. **a.** By 18, the sons and daughters would typically have reached their full heights. Younger people could be in different stages of growth and so not be directly comparable to their parents.

   **b.** Answers will vary. Sample response: Companies that make clothes, cars, airplanes, and buildings might want to know if people are getting taller. These companies may want to adjust the sizes of the things they make.

## Hints and Comments

### Overview

Students are introduced to the context of collecting data on peoples' heights.

### About the Mathematics

The mathematics in this section involves exploring a large data set, sampling, and determining whether a sample is chosen in a proper way (representativeness).

### Did You Know?

Many homes from early colonial times had only one room. With the help of other settlers, families constructed their homes themselves by felling trees, building frames, and installing fireplaces and chimneys.

Roofs were steep, and windows were small and placed high in the wall, the sill about four feet from the floor. All furniture was homemade, and most was heavy and simple. Often, homes had only one chair, plus stools or long benches that were too narrow to be good resting places.

Tables were long and could fold to conserve space during the day. Beds, also, had hinges near the head so they could be raised out of the way. One type of bed, a "jack bed," didn't fold and instead was built into one corner of the home. It was high off the floor and much shorter than beds are today because people did not sleep lying flat—they reclined in a half-sitting position.

## Are People Getting Taller?

### Notes

It is helpful for students to spend some time looking at the data before they begin problem 2. Point out the small numbers beside the data points and help students understand how those can be used to identify particular data pairs.

**3b** Students will probably say that problem 2d was the hardest because the answer is so far down the list. Ask the students if this indicates anything about whether fathers or sons are taller.

**4** Students' reflection about this problem will provide a framework for discussing the ideas that follow. Before moving on, challenge students to really think about what the statisticians might have done.

## The Pearson and Lee Data

The heights, in inches, of 1,064 pairs of fathers and sons from the Pearson and Lee data are listed in **Appendix A** at the end of this book. These data were reconstructed from Pearson and Lee's study.

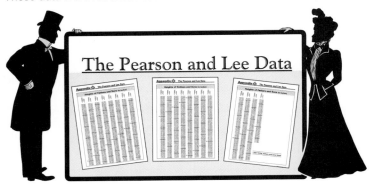

If you need to work with a long list of numbers, it helps to explore the data first.

2. From the data set in **Appendix A**, find the following:

    a. an example of a son who was at least 6 inches taller than his father

    b. an example of a father and son with the same height

    c. an example of a son who was shorter than his father

    d. an example of a son who was at least 6 inches shorter than his father

3. a. Which one of the examples in problem 2 was easy to find? Why?

    b. Which was the most difficult?

By studying the data, Pearson and Lee concluded that sons grow to be taller than their fathers.

4. **Reflect**  Describe what you think Pearson and Lee did with the data in order to reach their conclusion.

### Assessment Pyramid

Understand the need to organize and summarize a large data set in order for it to be useful.

### Reaching All Learners

**Intervention**

Students may be overwhelmed by the amount of data presented. Have students who are struggling with the data set focus on only one page, or even a single column. Some students may find it useful to use an index card to track through the list so that they can look at each pair of numbers one at a time.

**Advanced Learners**

Students could be challenged to use a small subset of the data to try their ideas from problem 4 to see how well they would work.

## Solutions and Samples

**2.** Answers will vary. Sample responses:

|  | Father | Son |
|---|---|---|
| **a.** | 64.0 | 71.0 (1st column, #18) |
| **b.** | 67.5 | 67.5 (1st column, #6) |
| **c.** | 70.0 | 67.8 (1st column, #4) |
| **d.** | 67.2 | 60.9 (3rd column, #129) |

**3. a.** Problems 2b and 2c are easy to answer because examples occur so early in the list in Appendix A.

   **b.** Students will probably say problem 2d was the most difficult because the first example is so far down the list in Appendix A.

**4.** Answers will vary. Sample response:

Pearson and Lee probably used strategies such as counting the cases in which the sons were taller than their fathers.

Other students may say that they made a graph or used a statistic, such as the mean (average) studied later in the unit.

## Hints and Comments

### Overview

Students investigate and describe the large data set of Pearson and Lee about the heights of fathers and sons.

### About the Mathematics

Sometimes a question requires one set of data and sometimes two. Two data sets are used here since students will be comparing fathers' and sons' heights. Also, the data sets are paired, which means that each value in one data set is related to a value in the other data set (a father's height, a son's height). Organizing data, especially large amounts of data, is an important skill. There are simply too many entries in Appendix A to get an idea of what trends may exist just by looking at the numbers, so there is a need for summarizing the data and representing them in different ways. Another important skill is skimming the data in order to get a first impression.

### Planning

Students may continue working in small groups on problems 2–4. Before they begin problem 2, you may want to tell them where to find the data gathered by Pearson and Lee (Appendix A, page 56–58 of the Student Book). Students will need these data for the problems in the rest of this section. After students have completed problem 4, you may want to have a brief class discussion about the data set.

### Comments About the Solutions

**2.** There are two purposes of this exercise. One is to learn to organize a search systematically. The other is for students to experience the huge size of this sample and the need for some method that will help them make sense of it.

**2. d.** Answering problem 2d should give students a sense of how uncommon it was to have a son who was much shorter than his father.

**3. b.** Discuss the answer from the Solutions column. You may wish to ask, *Does this tell you anything about which group was taller?* It is also possible to discuss the general impression students get from the data set by asking, *What do the data tell you?*

**4.** The goal is for students to understand the need for some organizing techniques. This question may give you some idea of what your students already know about the nature of statistics and the techniques used to organize data. You may want to refer to the unit *Picturing Numbers*.

# Are People Getting Taller?

## Notes

Be sure the students first compare the statements of Dustin and Anita, and then compare the statements of Anita and Tiwanda, before they compare all four statements. This allows the students to carefully consider each of the statements and the individual merits.

**5b** Note that Tiwanda's statement is the first step in calculating the mean, which is pulled up or down by very high or very low values (known as *outliers*).

**5c** Huong's statement is the most powerful, but it is not necessary for students to realize that at this point.

Four students studied the data from **Appendix A**. They all came to the conclusion that the sons were generally taller than their fathers. Here are their reasons (and everything they say is true).

Dustin says, "I know that the sons were generally taller than their fathers, because the tallest son in the data set was taller than the tallest father."

Anita says, "Overall, I say that the sons were taller, because more than half of them were."

Tiwanda says, "I can say that the sons were generally taller than their fathers, because the total height of all of the fathers is 72,033 inches. The total height of all of the sons is 73,126 inches."

Huong says, "The sons were taller than their fathers, in general, because in the data, sons were taller than their fathers 664 times out of 1,064 times. There were 19 ties."

5. **a.** Compare Dustin's and Anita's statements. Whose reasoning do you think better supports the statement "The sons grew to be taller than their fathers"? Why?

   **b.** Now compare Anita's and Tiwanda's statements. Which is more convincing?

   **c.** Which of the four statements would you use as an argument? Why?

## Assessment Pyramid

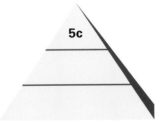

5c

Develop a critical attitude toward using statistical methods to solve problems and make a decision.

## Reaching All Learners

**Act It Out**

Students can play the role of each of the four students, reading their statements and even arguing that their idea is the best.

**Extension**

You might ask, *Which of the four students do you think used a calculator or computer?* (Probably Anita, Tiwanda, and Huong.)

# Solutions and Samples

**5.** Dustin: Dustin's argument is based on only one value. There is no way to tell what the trend is for all of the other values.

Anita: Anita makes good use of counting here. Most of the sons are taller than the fathers. Here the simple strategy of counting becomes a powerful tool. Her argument seems more convincing than Dustin's or Tiwanda's and is a simpler version of Huong's statement.

Tiwanda: Although Tiwanda is taking all of the data into account, her numbers might be misleading if there are several very tall sons.

Huong: He uses the same basic strategy as Anita, but his report is more specific.

**a.** Anita's reasoning supports the statement better than Dustin's. (See explanation above.)

**b.** Anita's reasoning can be considered better than Tiwanda's. (See explanation above.)

**c.** Answers will vary. Any of the four statements can be used, but some show more sophisticated reasoning than others. Also see the Hints and Comments column.

# Hints and Comments

## Overview

Students compare several statements about the Pearson and Lee data.

## About the Mathematics

A statistic is a number that summarizes a set of data. It may be a count, a representative value in a set of data, or an arithmetic combination of data points. Mean, median, and mode are examples of these. (They are introduced later in this unit.)

Statistics are used to make sense of data that would be impossible to understand without some organizing or summarizing techniques. Statistics and graphs work together in any data analysis. Graphs give you a visual picture of the data, and statistics summarize the data in two ways; they tell you about typical values and about the spread of the data. Sampling is discussed on the next page.

## Planning

You can have students work on problem 5 in small groups. Please encourage them to discuss their findings in the groups.

## Comments About the Solutions

**5.** This problem is designed to get students to see that statistics, even those as simple as counts, make arguments much more convincing. Good criteria for statistics include taking all of the data into account, reducing the complexity of the data to a few numbers, and using proportional reasoning.

**c.** Huong's method takes all the data into account and is stronger than Tiwanda's because it compares each pair rather than just group totals (which can be affected by a few extreme values).

# **A** Are People Getting Taller?

**Notes**

**6** This is the first time students are asked to think beyond the data set to the whole population. It is the first time they are asked to think explicitly about representativeness.

Therefore, this problem is critical. Questions such as *How many people would you have asked? Why?* may help students understand how sampling works and why it can be a good idea to sample rather than ask the entire population. Students may answer that it is the *size* of the sample that is important, while others may say that representativeness is most important. Give students time to think and discuss. Try to keep the discussion as open as possible.

## The Pearson and Lee Sample

Pearson and Lee were convinced that they had enough data.

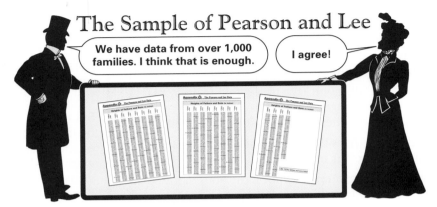

The Sample of Pearson and Lee

We have data from over 1,000 families. I think that is enough.

I agree!

**6.** How could this be when they knew that there were many fathers and sons for whom they had no data?

The group of families that Pearson and Lee studied is called a **sample**. A sample is a group taken from the whole population.

## **Reaching All Learners**

**Vocabulary Building**

*Sample* is a term that students may be familiar with, but it is important that they understand that it has a particular meaning within a statistical context. As stated in the Student Book, "A sample is a group taken from the whole population."

**Hands-On Learning**

To help students understand that very small samples are unlikely to be representative, you can fill a bag with multi-colored chips (or candies). Draw one and declare that you know the bag must be full of only the color you drew. Help students realize that you need more than one but fewer than the whole bag to have a good idea of what is in the bag.

## Solutions and Samples

**6.** Pearson and Lee collected data from a large sample. If chosen carefully, a large sample can reflect the whole population, even though the whole population may be much larger than the sample. Students may answer that it is the size of a sample that is important, while others may say that the way the sample is chosen is most important. Give students time to think and discuss here. Try to keep the discussion as open as possible to many different types of student responses.

## Hints and Comments

### Materials

colored chips or candies, optional

### Overview

Students think about the sample of Pearson and Lee in relation to the whole population. Students explore how to get a fair sample of a large population.

### About the Mathematics

On this page, some important terms are introduced. A *sample* is "a selection of a large group." The large group is often called *the population*. To be able to make valid statements about a population by looking only at the sample, the sample must be chosen in a proper way. This is an informal way of discussing the representativeness of a sample. The term *representative sample* is not used. Students should develop a critical attitude about surveys and how data are collected. The terms introduced on this page are revisited in the unit *Insights into Data*.

### Comments About the Solutions

**6.** This is the first time students are asked to think beyond the data set to the whole population of which it is a part.

## Notes

This page helps students understand that a sample needs to be representative.

**7** Some students may need help thinking about this problem. Begin by asking who was in the sample. Then ask questions to help students think about whether college students would have been representative of all of the people in England at the time.

### Activity

Students may need some help in thinking of mother-daughter pairs they can ask. Suggestions include mothers and grandmothers, and aunts and grandmothers. Remind students that the mothers and daughters must be genetically related. It is helpful to put the class data into a table or spreadsheet for safekeeping and future use.

## Sampling

To make valid conclusions about the whole population, the person gathering the data must choose a sample in a proper way. Conclusions from the sample about the characteristic they are studying, such as height, eye color, or favorite food, must also be true for the whole population. If the process of sampling is not carefully done, then the results are unreliable.

Pearson and Lee collected their data in England in 1903 by asking college students to measure the heights of their own family members and of people in other families they knew.

7. Do you think the Pearson and Lee sample was chosen in a proper way? Do you think the conclusions are valid for everyone in England at that time?

 **Activity**

You and your classmates can collect some current data to see how heights in families might be related today.

Find the heights of some mother-daughter pairs. Remember that the daughters should be at least 18 years old. Then gather all of the data from your classmates.

Use your data on mother-daughter pairs for the following problems.

- Make a list of the heights of the mother-daughter pairs collected by your classmates. Organize your data like the list in **Appendix A**.

- Make some statements about the data you collected.

## Assessment Pyramid

**Activity**

Collect, organize, and interpret data in tabular form.

## Reaching All Learners

### Advanced Learners

Students could be challenged to think up populations that their class is and is not representative of. For example, the class may be representative of sixth grade students in your city but not of sixth graders nationally. Encourage students to be specific about why their class is or is not a representative sample of a given population.

### Parent Involvement

Parents can help students in gathering mother-daughter data. In addition to family members, they may be able to ask coworkers, neighbors, and friends.

# Solutions and Samples

**7.** Answers will vary. Sample response:

College students in 1903 might not be typical of all people in England at that time. Good nutrition and health care might make a difference in people's heights, and at that time, people who went to the university were, in general, people from the upper social classes.

### Activity

- Answers (the lists) will vary depending on student data.

- Answers will vary. Students might give the minimum and maximum heights, the range, or the most common height. They can also make statements about mothers and daughters similar to those made on Student Book page 3 about the father and son data. Some might want to calculate the mean. (This will be studied later in this unit.) Students will probably find that, in general, daughters are taller than their mothers.

## Extension

You may wish to discuss how tall people are in general. The data on human heights given below can be used to stimulate discussion.

Women:

Minimum: 2 ft, 0.0 in.

Maximum: 8 ft, 1.8 in.

Mean (U.S.): 5 ft, 3.75 in.

Men:

Minimum: 1 ft, 10.5 in.

Maximum: 8 ft, 11.1 in.

Mean (U.S.): 5 ft, 9 in.

# Hints and Comments

### Materials

Blank transparency

### Overview

Students think about the sample of Pearson and Lee in relation to the whole population. Students explore how to get a fair sample of a large population.

### Planning

Students can work on problem 7 in small groups, discuss their answers in class. Students begin the activity by collecting data at home. They can then process their data in class the next day and finish the activity individually. Before you assign the activity, discuss with students whom they will ask (neighbors, older sisters, baby-sitters). If each student collects two pairs of data, that should be enough to see any patterns when students analyze the data (There is no minimum or maximum number of values that is "best.") Do not duplicate any mother-daughter pairs in the data collected and pooled by the students. Record all the information on a transparency, having the students call out the pairs of data they collected. This is a good opportunity to talk informally about "order" in ordered pairs.

### Comments About the Solutions

**7.** The reasoning of the students is more important than the answers they give. In problems 6 (page 4) and 7, it is the first time students are asked to think explicitly about how samples are chosen.

### Activity

The data collection must be done as homework. It is possible that someone at age 18 would not have reached full height, but the idea is to use the same methods used by Pearson and Lee. Make sure you keep the data handy—it will be used throughout the unit.

### Interdisciplinary Connection

Surveys are conducted in many areas and fields. Newspapers and magazines often publish the results of surveys without telling how the survey was organized. Students should develop a critical attitude toward surveys.

**Are People Getting Taller?**

## Notes

The Summary for this section reiterates the idea of samples and the importance of organizing a large data set. It is helpful to read the Summary aloud.

Be sure to go over the Check Your Work problems with students so that they learn when their answer is correct, even if it does not exactly match the answer given.

**For Further Reflection**

Reflective questions are meant to summarize important concepts from the section.

 **Are People Getting Taller?**

### Summary

When people are investigating a question, they usually collect data. If the group they want to study is very big, the investigators often take a *sample* because they cannot ask everyone in the group.

It is important to be sure that the sample is chosen in a proper way; otherwise, conclusions can be wrong.

A long list of data is better understood if it is organized. To understand data, you need to think about the numbers carefully in some systematic way.

### Check Your Work

1. Why is it important to choose a sample in a proper way?

2. Ann wants to know which sports students like. She decides to ask students on Saturday in the swimming pool. Do you think she chose the sample in a proper way?

3. Why is a long list of data hard to describe?

4. What might you do to organize a large data set?

### For Further Reflection

Scientists have decided to investigate the heights of fathers and sons today. Describe how you think they should choose their sample. Write the differences and similarities you might expect to find between this data and the data from Pearson and Lee. Be specific in your explanations.

## Assessment Pyramid

3, 4

1, 2, ☐FFR

Assesses Section A Goals

## Reaching All Learners

**Parent Involvement**

Have student "teach" their parents about sampling. The family could think of a population that they are representative of.

**Extension**

Students could give Ann (from problem 2) suggestions about where she might ask her questions to get a more representative sample.

## Solutions and Samples

### Answers to Check Your Work

1. If a sample is not chosen in a proper way, the data may not give a true picture of the population.

2. No, people in a swimming pool will probably answer "swimming" as a sport they like. People who don't like swimming would not be at the pool.

3. If there are many numbers, it is difficult to see patterns, clusters, or trends. The data have to be organized and summarized in some way.

4. You can do different things to organize the data. For example, you can:
   - put the data in order from least to greatest;
   - plot the data on a graph; or
   - calculate the mean and the range to summarize the data.

### For Further Reflection

Answers will vary. Students will note that in general a similarity is that sons are usually taller than their fathers. A difference may be that the values for the heights are different. Nowadays people are taller than they were around 1900.

## Hints and Comments

### Overview

Students read the Summary and do the problems on this page. In doing so they review the main mathematical concepts and skills addressed in this section.

### Planning

After students complete Section A, you may assign as homework appropriate activities from the Additional Practice section, located on Student Book page 46.

### Extension

Students might bring to class clippings about surveys from magazines or newspapers. Ask them to consider whether the sample is described and whether it seems to be representative.

### Did You Know?

Medical studies often use unrepresentative samples; in fact, most early medical research included only men.

## Section Focus

Students learn to make a scatter plot by plotting matched pairs on a coordinate system. They then examine and evaluate the complete scatter plot of the Pearson and Lee data on the heights of fathers and their sons.

## Pacing and Planning

| Day 3: Graphs and Tables | | Student pages 7–9 |
|---|---|---|
| INTRODUCTION | Problem 1 | Plot father-son height data on a scatter plot. |
| CLASSWORK | Problems 2–4 | Interpret points on a scatter plot of the father-son data. |
| HOMEWORK | Problem 5 | Use the scatter plot to identify initial trends in the father-son data. |

| Day 4: Graphs and Tables (Continued) | | Student pages 9–11 |
|---|---|---|
| INTRODUCTION | Review homework. | Review homework from Day 3. |
| CLASSWORK | Problems 6–10 | Analyze scatter plot data and create a scatter plot of mother-daughter height data. |
| HOMEWORK | Check Your Work and For Further Reflection | Student self-assessment: Create, interpret, and analyze data on a scatter plot. |

| Day 4: Graphs and Tables (Continued) | | Student pages 9–11 |
|---|---|---|
| INTRODUCTION | Review homework. | Review homework from Day 4. |
| ASSESSMENT | Quiz 1 | Assessment of Section A and B Goals |

Additional Resources: *Additional Practice*, Section B, Student Book page 47

## Materials

### Student Resources

Quantities listed are per student.

- **Student Activity Sheets 1–3**

### Teachers Resources

No resources required

### Student Materials

Quantities listed are per student.

- Colored pencils—red, blue, and green
- Ruler or straightedge

\* See Hints and Comments for optional materials.

## Learning Lines

### Organizing and Representing Large Data Sets

This section introduces students to the scatter plot.

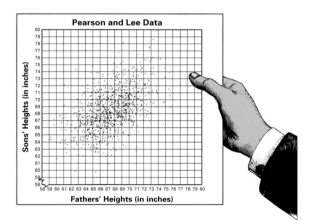

Each point on a scatter plot represents one data pair. Students learn how to make a scatter plot on a coordinate grid. They have made graphs on a coordinate system in the unit *Expressions and Formulas*; the coordinate system will be formally introduced in the unit *Operations*.

Students learn to interpret a scatter plot and draw conclusions from it about the data. Scatter plots are useful in seeing patterns in the data and finding clusters or identifying trends or outliers (points whose values or coordinates are considerably different from those of all the other points). Students learn to think carefully about the plots and about what a given point represents.

The $y = x$ line, through all points whose coordinates are equal, can help students make inferences about the data. This line is defined in terms of the situation: in this case it is the line where each son's height equals his fathers' height. This line can help to see which group was taller. Any data points representing pairs in which sons were taller than their fathers will be on one side of the line. Data points for pairs in which fathers were taller will be on the other (opposite) side.

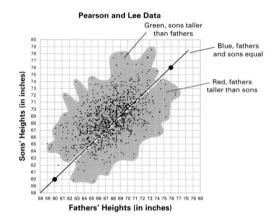

Scatter plots are further studied in the unit *Insights into Data*.

### At the End of This Section: Learning Outcomes

Students will:

- be able to plot points to create a scatter plot from paired data;
- understand and interpret scatter plots; and
- understand the meaning of the line $y = x$ in a scatter plot if this line is defined in terms of the situation.

## Notes

This page will take more or less time depending on students' previous experiences with plotting points.

**1** By convention, the first number in an ordered pair is the horizontal coordinate, and the second number is the vertical coordinate. Students do not need to use formal notation at this point. The dotted lines are imaginary and are used to guide students in locating the point. Students who need more help may draw the lines when plotting points *B* through *E*.

**1c** This question is intended to get students to think about how the graph might help answer the question.

**B**

# Scatter Plots

## Graphs and Tables

Graphs and tables help you see patterns and trends in long lists of data.

Pearson and Lee wanted to make a graph that would help them understand more about the relationship between the heights of fathers and sons.

Shown here are the heights of five pairs of fathers and sons, taken from the Pearson and Lee data.

|   | Fathers' Heights (in inches) | Sons' Heights (in inches) |
|---|---|---|
| **A** | 66.8 | 68.4 |
| **B** | 68.5 | 69.4 |
| **C** | 65.6 | 67.5 |
| **D** | 70.0 | 67.8 |
| **E** | 67.5 | 67.5 |

You can plot the heights of each father-son pair with a point on the grid on **Student Activity Sheet 1**.

The heights of all of the fathers and sons range from 58 to 80 inches.

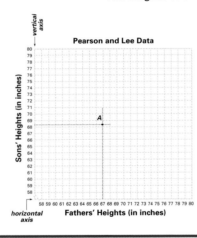

The scale along the bottom of the graph is called the **horizontal axis**. Another scale is marked off on a line that goes up and down on the paper. This is called the **vertical axis**.

The graph shows the location of point *A*, which corresponds to the father-son pair *A* at (66.8, 68.4).

1. **a.** Put this point on the grid on **Student Activity Sheet 1**. Explain how you plotted this point.

   **b.** Plot points *B, C, D,* and *E* on the grid on **Student Activity Sheet 1**.

   **c.** What statement can you make about the heights of fathers and sons from the points you plotted?

---

## Reaching All Learners

### Intervention

Students who have difficulty graphing could be asked to round the values to whole numbers (or be given the numbers already rounded) to make the graphing easier. Larger graph paper may be useful as well.

Students could choose five additional points from the data set to plot.

# Solutions and Samples

**1. a.** Explanations will vary. Sample explanation:

The height of father *A* is 66.8 inches. I found this on the horizontal axis (Fathers' Heights). Then I lightly drew a vertical line from this point.

The height of the son is 68.4 inches. I found this on the vertical axis (Sons' Heights). Then I lightly drew a horizontal line from this point.

I placed a point where the two lines cross. The point stands for the father-and-son pair where the father is 66.8 inches and the son is 68.4 inches tall.

**b.** See scatter plot below.

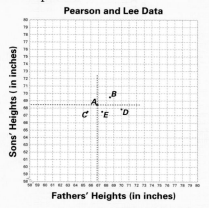

The points can be described as follows:

(Father's height, Son's height)

Point A  (66.8, 68.4)

Point B  (68.5, 69.4)

Point C  (65.6, 67.5)

Point D  (70.0, 67.8)

Point E  (67.5, 67.5)

**c.** Answers may vary. Sample student answers: For four out of the five cases plotted, the son is as tall as or taller than the father. For these cases: taller fathers have taller sons.

The five points in the graph do not show a clear pattern; they are in a kind of cloud.

# Hints and Comments

## Materials

**Student Activity Sheet 1** (one per student) large graph paper, optional

## Overview

Students study the father-son heights in more detail and plot the data as ordered pairs on a graph.

## About the Mathematics

A grid with a horizontal axis and a vertical axis is called a *coordinate system*. This term is formally introduced in the unit *Operations*. The different aspects of the axes (whether they show an origin, the scaling, and so forth) are also studied in more detail in the unit *Insights into Data*.

## Planning

You may start this section by explaining how to organize the large data set of Pearson and Lee. You can refresh students' knowledge of plotting ordered pairs as points. Students do not need to know the term *coordinate system* yet; however, you may want to mention it. Students may work on problem 1 as a class activity.

## Comments About the Solutions

**1. a.** Although students may understand the general procedure for plotting points, encourage them not to draw lines to plot each point. (See the Solutions column.)

**Notes**

If you plot all 1,064 pairs of data that are in **Appendix A**, on the grid on **Student Activity Sheet 1**, you would get the diagram below. It is called a **scatter plot**. The points are "scattered" across the diagram. By making a scatter plot, you create a picture of your data.

**2** This is a good question with which to assess students' understanding of coordinate graphs. Remind students that whenever they make a plot or graph, they should label the axes and give the graph a title.

**3** It is helpful to use a copy of **Student Activity Sheet 2** on a transparency and have students show which points go with each question as the discussion proceeds.

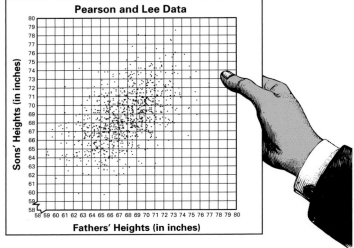

Pearson and Lee Data

Sons' Heights (in inches)

Fathers' Heights (in inches)

2. The numbers along the axes of the scatter plot start with 58, not 0. Why is this?

Use the copy of the scatter plot on **Student Activity Sheet 2** for problems 3–7.

3. **a.** Circle the point that represents the tallest father. How tall is he? How tall is his son? Is he the tallest son?

   **b.** Circle the point that represents the shortest father. How tall is he? Is he taller than his son? How does the height of his son compare to the heights of the other sons?

## Reaching All Learners

**Vocabulary Building**

A scatter plot is defined on this page. A technical definition of a *scatter plot* is a plot of two-variable data where the horizontal and vertical axes each represent one of the related values.

# Solutions and Samples

2. All of the fathers and sons were taller than 58 inches. If the scales started at zero, the lower left part of the grid would be empty, and the horizontal and vertical lines would be so close together that it would be hard to be accurate for the small part that contained the data (unless you used a very large piece of paper).

3. **a.** The tallest father is about 76.5 inches (the point farthest right), and his son is about 72.4 inches. The tallest son is about 78.6 inches. The tallest father does not have the tallest son.

   **b.** The shortest father is about 59.0 inches tall (the point farthest left), and his son is about 65.1 inches tall. This is shorter than most other sons.

# Hints and Comments

## Materials

**Student Activity Sheets 1 and 2** (one of each per student);
transparency of **Student Activity Sheet 2**, optional (one per class)

## Overview

Students investigate a scatter plot of the Pearson and Lee data.

## About the Mathematics

The term *scatter plot* is introduced on this page. In a scatter plot, the points are scattered all over the grid. Each point on the grid represents a data point. In this section, students will learn how to make and use a scatter plot. To make a scatter plot students must plot points on a grid.

## Planning

You may wish to make a transparency of **Student Activity Sheet 2** for use with problems 3–7.

## Comments About the Solutions

2. Student use of coordinate graphs will be formally addressed in other units, for example, the unit *Operations*.

## Notes

**5** This question is critical. It is the first time students are asked to look at the scatter plot in a more global way rather than looking at individual points.

**6** and **7** After students plot their own graphs, have them make a class graph on an overhead transparency if possible. Have each student mark a number of points of each color and have the class look at the graph periodically so that they can see the pattern emerge.

A good question to ask here is, *What would the scatter plot look like if there were no relationship between fathers' and sons' heights?* (The points would be scattered all over the graph.)

**4. a.** Find a point that seems to be in the center of the cloud of points. What are the father's and son's heights for this point?

  **b.** What does this point tell you?

Dustin says, "From the graph, it looks like the taller the father is, the taller the son is."

**5. Reflect** Do you agree? Explain your reasoning.

**6. a.** Find three points for which sons are taller than their fathers. Circle these points with a green pencil.

  **b.** Find three points for which fathers are taller than their sons. Circle these points with a red pencil.

  **c.** Combine the class's results on one graph. What patterns can you see?

**7. a.** Find some points on the graph for which fathers are as tall as their sons. Circle these points with a blue pencil.

  **b.** What do you notice about how these points lie on the graph?

  **c.** Study the graph you just colored. What can you say about the heights of the fathers compared to the heights of the sons?

**8.** On **Student Activity Sheet 3**, make a scatter plot of the class data that you collected for mothers and daughters in Section A.

**9. a.** Find some points on your plot that represent mothers and daughters who are equal in height. Draw a line through these points.

  **b.** What does it mean if a point lies above this line?

  **c.** What does it mean if a point lies below the line?

  **d.** What does it mean if a point lies very far from the line?

**10. Reflect** What possible conclusions can you make based on your data of mothers' and daughters' heights? Write an argument to support your conclusions.

## Assessment Pyramid

**6ab**

Interpret a scatter plot from paired data.

## Reaching All Learners

**Parent Involvement**

Students could show their parents their mother-daughter plot and show where the people they contributed fall within the data set.

**Intervention**

Students could be given a graph with some of the points already colored for problem 6 and then be asked to find more points like those.

**English Language Learners**

Dustin's statement may be hard for students to understand. It can be reworded more simply as, "Tall fathers have tall sons, and short fathers have short sons."

## Solutions and Samples

**4. a.** Answers will vary. The middle may be at (or around) one of the following locations: (68,69), (68,70), (69,69), and (69,70). In most cases, the son is taller than the father.

**b.** The point (father's height, son's height) that shows the center suggests that sons may be taller than fathers overall.

**5.** Answers will vary. Sample response:

There is a pattern of points starting in the lower left and moving to the upper right. This upward pattern on the graph shows that few tall fathers have short sons and that few short fathers have tall sons. So the height of a son is related to the height of his father.

**6. a.** These points are above the diagonal line in the graph shown below.

**b.** These points are below the diagonal line in the graph shown below.

**c.** Answers may vary. Students may say that the green area is separated from the red area by a line.

**7. a.** These points are on the diagonal line in the graph below.

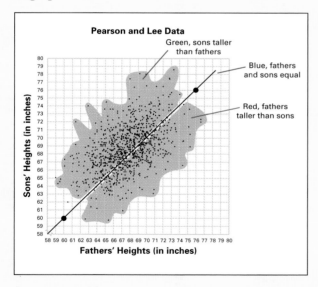

**b.** The points should lie on the diagonal line that splits the graph.

**c.** The green area seems to have more points. This shows that there are more sons who are taller than their fathers than vice versa.

**8.** Answers will vary, depending on the data collected by the class.

## Hints and Comments

### Materials

transparency of **Student Activity Sheet 2**, optional (one per class);
overhead projector, optional (one per class);
**Student Activity Sheet 3** (one per student);
red, green, and blue pencils (one of each per student);
ruler or straightedge (one per student)

### Overview

Students continue the investigation of the scatter plot. They make a scatter plot for the data they collected regarding mothers' and daughters' heights.

### About the Mathematics

The center of a scatter plot can be used as a summary value to describe the whole set of data. The diagonal line running from the lower left corner to the upper right corner of the graph is the line where each son's height equals his father's height.

Students should be able to describe the scatter plot in their own words. A scatter plot is a good graphical representation for exploring patterns in data. If there is a linear relationship between the two variables, the shape of the cloud of data points is an indicator of how strong this relationship is. The closer the data points are to the line, the stronger the indication that there is a linear relationship between the two variables.

Linear relationships between two variables are studied explicitly in the unit *Insights into Data*. This unit lays the foundation for future study of more formal notations.

**9. a.** Answers will vary, but for each point chosen the horizontal value and the vertical value should be equal. If the scales on both axes begin at the same value, the line drawn by students should be the diagonal that cuts the graph into two equal halves.

**b.** Points above this line represent pairs in which daughters are taller than their mothers.

**c.** Points below the line represent pairs in which mothers are taller than their daughters.

**d.** A point that is far from the line represents a pair in which there is a big difference in the heights of the mother and daughter.

**10.** Answers will vary. Students may conclude that the taller the mother, the taller the daughter. In general, daughters are taller than their mothers.

## Notes

Reading the Summary as a class can be helpful to make sure that all students know the important ideas in the section.

**1d** Encourage students to think about what they notice about how many points fall into each of the categories defined in parts **a, b,** and **c** before they answer part **d**.

**B** Scatter Plots

### Summary

Graphs of data can help you see patterns that you cannot see in a list of numbers. Looking at a picture, you can see the patterns in the data all at once.

A scatter plot is a good graph to use when you have two data sets that are paired in some way.

The graph on the right has data for mothers' and daughters' heights in inches.

Scatter plots can help you see features of the data, such as whether the tallest mother has the tallest daughter. Scatter plots can also reveal patterns.

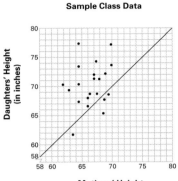

**Sample Class Data**

In scatter plots like those for the heights of parents and their children, you can draw a line through the points where members of pairs have the same value. This line can help you to see relationships.

### Check Your Work

1. In the graph in the Summary above, you see data of mothers' and daughters' heights in inches.

   **a.** What do the points above the dotted line indicate?

   **b.** What do the points on the dotted line indicate?

   **c.** What do the points below the dotted line indicate?

   **d.** Make a general statement about the height of mothers and daughters based on this graph.

## Reaching All Learners

### Bringing Math Home

As an informal assessment, you may ask students to look for a scatter plot in a magazine or newspaper and to describe it using the mathematics they learned in this section. This activity assesses students' ability to create and interpret a scatter plot from paired data.

### Extension

Ask students to list other data sets that are paired or that could be represented with a scatter plot. You might ask, *What are some other types of data that could be represented on a scatter plot? What information could you learn from comparing these data sets?*

## Solutions and Samples

### Answers to Check Your Work

1. **a.** Daughters taller than their mothers
   **b.** Daughters with the same height as their mothers
   **c.** Daughters shorter than their mothers
   **d.** Most daughters are taller than their mothers.

## Hints and Comments

### Materials

transparency of scatter plot for mother-daughter data

### Overview

Students read the Summary and do the problems on these pages. They reflect on Section B and summarize what they have learned about scatter plots.

### About the Mathematics

Plotting points, drawing lines, and interpreting and describing scatter plots are the mathematical skills students have learned in this section.

### Planning

The Bringing Math Home and Extension activities in the Reaching All Learners section on page 10 may be assigned as homework.

After students complete Section B, you may assign as homework appropriate activities from the Additional Practice section, located on Student Book page 47.

**Notes**

Athletes can measure their condition with a test called the Cooper test. They have to run as far as possible in exactly 12 minutes. Up to age eight, they run for six minutes.

In the table, you find the results for a group of girls between ages four and eight.

| Name | Age | Distance (in meters) |
|---|---|---|
| Rayna | 7 | 1,210 |
| Jacinta | 8 | 1,070 |
| Bridget | 6 | 1,020 |
| Kiyo | 8 | 960 |
| Keva | 7 | 910 |
| Ashley | 7 | 1,160 |
| Mila | 7 | 1,090 |
| Barb | 7 | 950 |
| MinJung | 8 | 900 |
| Daya | 6 | 770 |
| Yvinne | 4 | 620 |
| Maria | 5 | 600 |
| Coretta | 4 | 400 |
| Chris | 8 | 1,200 |
| Stacey | 5 | 730 |

**2a** Remind students to think about appropriate scales before beginning to make the graph.

**2b** The fact that the two variables have different scales may worry some students who want to use the line of equal values to interpret the graph. Encourage those students to look at the shape of the graph alone.

2. **a.** Make a scatter plot using the results in the table. Put the girls' ages on the horizontal axis.

   **b.** Write three conclusions based on your graph.

 **For Further Reflection**

**For Further Reflection**

Reflective questions are meant to summarize important concepts from the section.

Describe how a scatter plot helps or does not help you understand something about the data the plot represents. Use data sets from Sections A and B to illustrate what you mean.

**Assessment Pyramid**

☒ FFR

2ab

Assesses Section B Goals

## Reaching All Learners

**Extension**

Students could create a scatter plot of their own data. Possibilities include distance lived from school vs. time to get to school, their own weight vs. height at birth, and their hand span vs. their foot length.

# Solutions and Samples

**2. a.**

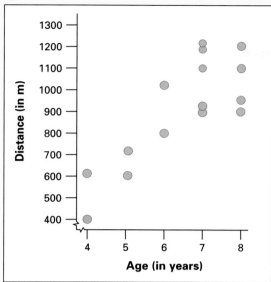

**b.** You may have many different statements. Sample responses:

- In general, it looks like the older you are, the longer the distance you run.

- The girl (Rayna) running the largest distance (1,210 m) is not the oldest one in the group; she is only 7 years old.

- The girl running the shortest distance is one of the two youngest ones in the group

### For Further Reflection

Answers will vary. Sample answer:

A scatter plot can help you see patterns or trends in a set of data and can reveal outliers. A scatter plot is not very helpful if you need to find the mean.

### Overview

Students reflect on Section B and summarize what they have learned about scatter plots.

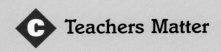 **Teachers Matter**

## Section Focus

Students represent data using dot plots, stem-and-leaf plots, and histograms, and use these plots to answer questions about the data. The mode is formally introduced in this section. Students use a data set of the ages of U.S. presidents at inauguration, as well as the data set of Pearson and Lee about the heights of fathers and sons. Students also collect and explore their own data set on estimates of the size of the teacher's head.

## Pacing and Planning

| Day 6: Stem-and-Leaf Plots | | Student pages 12–15 |
|---|---|---|
| INTRODUCTION | Problems 1–3 | Identify the youngest and oldest presidents from a table of data. |
| CLASSWORK | Problems 4–6 | Organize data on presidents' ages at inauguration. |
| HOMEWORK | Problems 7 and 8 | Compare a tally chart with a bar graph. |

| Day 7: Stem-and-Leaf Plots | | Student pages 16 and 17 |
|---|---|---|
| INTRODUCTION | Review homework. | Review homework from Day 6. |
| CLASSWORK | Problems 9 and 10 | Create a stem-and-leaf plot of the presidential data. |
| HOMEWORK | Problems 11–13 | Reorganize the stem-and-leaf plot to make it easier to read. |

| Day 8: Histogram | | Student pages 18 and 19 |
|---|---|---|
| INTRODUCTION | Problem 14 | Compare a histogram to a stem-and-leaf plot and collect data on the length of a teacher's head (see homework). |
| CLASSWORK | Problems 15 and 16 | Compare three different histograms of the Pearson and Lee data. |
| HOMEWORK | Activity: Page 18 | Make a histogram of the data collected on the estimates of the length of the teacher's head. |

| Day 9: Histogram (Continued) | | Student pages 20–24 |
|---|---|---|
| INTRODUCTION | Problem 17 | Compare father-son height data using a histogram. |
| CLASSWORK | Problem 18 | Create a stem-and-leaf plot and a histogram of the mother-daughter data. |
| HOMEWORK | Check Your Work and For Further Reflection | Student self-assessment of Section C goals. |

Additional Resources: Additional Practice, Section C, Student Book page 48

## Materials

### Student Resources

No resource required

### Teachers Resources

No resources required

### Student Materials

Quantities listed are per student.

- Graph paper (two sheets)
- Measuring tape
- Ruler or straightedge

* See Hints and Comments for optional materials.

## Learning Lines

### Organizing Large Data Sets

Students study the data set of the ages of U.S. presidents at inauguration. This data set is presented as a large table. Finding specific information from the data set is easier if the information is ordered in some way. Students have seen this in Section A for the data set of Pearson and Lee. Students organize the president data in a new list or a diagram that makes it easier to see the distribution and to answers questions about the data.

### Representing Data in Graphs

This section introduces dot plots, frequency tables, stem-and-leaf plots, and histograms, offering examples using the presidents' ages at inauguration. Students have seen some of these types of graphs in the unit *Picturing Numbers*.

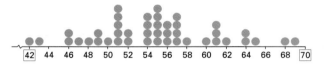

**Age at Inauguration**

## Using Statistics to Represent Data

Data sets can be represented using numbers that summarize them—that is, statistics. Students have been informally introduced to the measures of central tendency in the unit *Picturing Numbers*. In this section, students think about what typical number may represent the age of a president at inauguration. The mode (one of the common one-number summaries) is formally introduced in this section, as "the value that occurs most often." The other statistics commonly used are the mean (see Section D) and the median (see Section E).

### At the End of This Section: Learning Outcomes

Students will:

- understand the need to organize and summarize a large set of data in order for it to be useful;
- be able to create and interpret a stem-and-leaf plot and a histogram;
- be able to find and interpret the mode of a data set;
- compare different representations and understand their differences and similarities; and
- be able to build an argument based on statistical measures and graphs, specifically: they can use the mode and dot plots, stem-and-leaf-plots, and histograms.

These problems are not
about mathematics. They
are intended to help
students become familiar
with the context.

**1a** Students may not have
learned the qualifications
for U.S. presidents. The
president must be a U.S.
citizen born in the United
States and be 35 years old.

**C**

# Stem-and-Leaf Plots and Histograms

## Stem-and-Leaf Plots

Theodore Roosevelt was the youngest person to become president
of the United States. He was 42 at his inauguration. John F. Kennedy
was 43, making him the second youngest.

Theodore Roosevelt

John F. Kennedy

**1. a.** Is it possible for a 40-year-old to be president of the
United States?

**b. Reflect** How old do you think a president of the United States
should be?

Pages 13 and 14 show when all of the presidents of the United
States were born, when they were inaugurated as president,
and when they died.

**2.** Who was the oldest person ever to become president of
the United States?

---

### Reaching All Learners

**Vocabulary Building**

Students may not be familiar with the term *inauguration*, the point at
which the presidency changes.

# Solutions and Samples

**1. a.** It is possible for the president of the United States to be 40 years old. The Constitution requires the president to be at least 35 years old.

  **b.** Answers will vary. Sample responses:

    A president should be old enough to have experience, but not so old as to be too frail for the difficult work.

    The age of a president should not be considered, only the person's experience and ability to handle the job.

**2.** The oldest president was Ronald Reagan, who was 69.

# Hints and Comments

## Overview

Students are introduced to the context of this section, the age of the presidents at their inauguration. They explore a table that lists the presidents and their ages at inauguration.

## About the Mathematics

In this section, students will learn how to make and use a stem-and-leaf plot and a histogram. Systematically looking for specific information presented in a table is not always easy. One way to facilitate this is to order the information in such a way that the information can easily be found.

## Planning

You may introduce this section with a class discussion about presidents and inaugurations. Students may do problems 1 and 2 as a class.

## Interdisciplinary Connection

You can ask the history teacher for more information about the American presidents. Students may be able to share a great deal of information related to the presidents in a class discussion to begin this section.

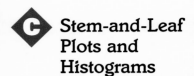

# Stem-and-Leaf Plots and Histograms

| Name | Born | Inaugurated | at Age | Died | at Age |
|---|---|---|---|---|---|
| George Washington | Feb. 22, 1732 | 1789 | 57 | Dec. 14, 1799 | 67 |
| John Adams | Oct. 30, 1735 | 1797 | 61 | Jul. 4, 1826 | 90 |
| Thomas Jefferson | Apr. 13, 1743 | 1801 | 57 | Jul. 4, 1826 | 83 |
| James Madison | Mar. 16, 1751 | 1809 | 57 | Jun. 28, 1836 | 85 |
| James Monroe | Apr. 28, 1758 | 1817 | 58 | Jul. 4, 1831 | 73 |
| John Q. Adams | Jul. 11, 1767 | 1825 | 57 | Feb. 23, 1848 | 80 |
| Andrew Jackson | Mar. 15, 1767 | 1829 | 61 | Jun. 8, 1845 | 78 |
| Martin Van Buren | Dec. 5, 1782 | 1837 | 54 | Jul. 24, 1862 | 79 |
| William H. Harrison | Feb. 9, 1773 | 1841 | 68 | Apr. 4, 1841 | 68 |
| John Tyler | Mar. 29, 1790 | 1841 | 51 | Jan. 18, 1862 | 71 |
| James K. Polk | Nov. 2, 1795 | 1845 | 49 | Jun. 15, 1849 | 53 |
| Zachary Taylor | Nov. 24, 1784 | 1849 | 64 | Jul. 9, 1850 | 65 |
| Millard Fillmore | Jan. 7, 1800 | 1850 | 50 | Mar. 8, 1874 | 74 |
| Franklin Pierce | Nov. 23, 1804 | 1853 | 48 | Oct. 8, 1869 | 64 |
| James Buchanan | Apr. 23, 1791 | 1857 | 65 | Jun. 1, 1868 | 77 |
| Abraham Lincoln | Feb. 12, 1809 | 1861 | 52 | Apr. 15, 1865 | 56 |
| Andrew Johnson | Dec. 29, 1808 | 1865 | 56 | Jul. 31, 1875 | 66 |
| Ulysses S. Grant | Apr. 27, 1822 | 1869 | 46 | Jul. 23, 1885 | 63 |
| Rutherford B. Hayes | Oct. 4, 1822 | 1877 | 54 | Jan. 17, 1893 | 70 |
| James A. Garfield | Nov. 19, 1831 | 1881 | 49 | Sep. 19, 1881 | 49 |
| Chester A. Arthur | Oct. 5, 1829 | 1881 | 51 | Nov. 18, 1886 | 57 |
| Grover Cleveland | Mar. 18, 1837 | 1885 | 47 | Jun. 24, 1908 | 71 |
| Benjamin Harrison | Aug. 20, 1833 | 1889 | 55 | Mar. 13, 1901 | 67 |
| Grover Cleveland | Mar. 18, 1837 | 1893 | 55 | Jun. 24, 1908 | 71 |
| William McKinley | Jan. 29, 1843 | 1897 | 54 | Sep. 14, 1901 | 58 |

## Reaching All Learners

**Accommodation**

A copy of the table with only the ages at inauguration may be helpful for students overwhelmed by the table as presented.

## Hints and Comments

### Did You Know?

Four United States presidents died of natural causes while in office. William Henry Harrison, nominated by conservatives who thought he would be easy to control, ran against Martin Van Buren twice and finally beat him in 1840. In a campaign speech in 1838, Harrison promised, among such things as regarding the laws of the people and not controlling the treasury, that he would "confine [his] service to a single term." Indeed, one month after inauguration, Harrison died from complications caused by pneumonia.

Zachary Taylor never voted in a presidential election before he was elected in 1848. Much of his work during his presidency focused on the issue of slavery in the South, but he died—supposedly from a gastronomic condition exacerbated by eating a bowl of cherries and drinking a pitcher of ice milk—before he fulfilled his agenda. Just before dying, Taylor said, "I regret nothing, but I am sorry that I am about to leave my friends."

Warren Gamaliel Harding was elected president in 1920. He served for two years before dying in office of unknown causes. Historians suppose that Harding may have died from complications caused by a stroke or pneumonia. Although Harding maintains a reputation of sound personal integrity, his Cabinet is infamous for its incompetence and corruption. Strangely, Harding once said, "Government is not of supermen, but of normal men, very much like you or me. . . ."

Franklin Delano Roosevelt became the 32nd president in 1932. He withstood four elections, one assassination attempt, and a bout with infantile paralysis. Several months after inauguration into his fourth term, Roosevelt died of a cerebral hemorrhage. About his presidency, he is famous for saying, "The first twelve years are the hardest."

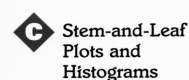
**Notes**

◆ Stem-and-Leaf Plots and Histograms

| | Name | Born | Inaugurated | at Age | Died | at Age |
|---|---|---|---|---|---|---|
| | Theodore Roosevelt | Oct. 27, 1858 | 1901 | 42 | Jan. 6, 1919 | 60 |
| | William H. Taft | Sep. 15, 1857 | 1909 | 51 | Mar. 8, 1930 | 72 |
| | Woodrow Wilson | Dec. 28, 1856 | 1913 | 56 | Feb. 3, 1924 | 67 |
| | Warren G. Harding | Nov. 2, 1865 | 1921 | 55 | Aug. 2, 1923 | 57 |
| | Calvin Coolidge | Jul. 4, 1872 | 1923 | 51 | Jan. 5, 1933 | 60 |
| | Herbert C. Hoover | Aug. 10, 1874 | 1929 | 54 | Oct. 20, 1964 | 90 |
| | Franklin D. Roosevelt | Jan. 30, 1882 | 1933 | 51 | Apr.12, 1945 | 63 |
| | Harry S. Truman | May 8, 1884 | 1945 | 60 | Dec. 26, 1972 | 88 |
| | Dwight D. Eisenhower | Oct. 14, 1890 | 1953 | 62 | Mar. 28, 1969 | 78 |
| | John F. Kennedy | May 29, 1917 | 1961 | 43 | Nov. 22, 1963 | 46 |
| | Lyndon B. Johnson | Aug. 27, 1908 | 1963 | 55 | Jan. 22, 1973 | 64 |
| | Richard M. Nixon* | Jan. 9, 1913 | 1969 | 56 | Apr. 22, 1994 | 81 |
| | Gerald R. Ford | Jul. 14, 1913 | 1974 | 61 | | |
| | James E. Carter | Oct. 1, 1924 | 1977 | 52 | | |
| | Ronald Reagan | Feb. 6, 1911 | 1981 | 69 | Jun. 5, 2004 | 93 |
| | George Bush | Jun. 12, 1924 | 1989 | 64 | | |
| | William J. Clinton | Aug. 19, 1946 | 1993 | 46 | | |
| | George W. Bush | Jul. 6, 1946 | 2001 | 54 | | |

*Resigned Aug. 9, 1974

Most of the presidents were from 50 to 54 years old at the time of inauguration.

**3.** **Reflect**   Do you agree with this student? Write down your reasons.

**3** Students will need to explore the data set in order to answer this question. The intent of the problem is for students to begin to see the need for a more systematic list or representation of the data.

## Reaching All Learners

**Extension**

Students could be asked to make a similar statement about the ages at which the presidents died. This should be informal at this point, and students can revise their statement as they explore the techniques in the section.

# Solutions and Samples

**3.** The student's statement is incorrect. There were 13 presidents who were ages 50 to 54 when they were inaugurated, but there were also 12 presidents who were ages 55 to 59. A better description of the data would be that most presidents were between 50 and 60 at the time of their inauguration.

# Hints and Comments

## Overview

Students continue exploring the U.S. presidents' data set and comment on a statement summarizing the data.

## About the Mathematics

Statements about a large data set are harder to check if data are not organized in some way. In the rest of this section, the data set will be organized in several ways.

## Planning

You can have students work on problem 3 in small groups.

## Comments About the Solutions

**3.** You may wish to have students explore the U.S. presidents' data set a little more before trying to answer this problem. The intent of the problem is for students to begin to see the need for a more systematic list or representation of the data.

# Stem-and-Leaf Plots and Histograms

## Notes

It may be helpful to pose problem 4 aloud before students look at the page so students do not think that the dot plot shown below is the only correct possibility.

**5** Note: Grover Cleveland is listed twice and counted twice in this number line plot. He was the 22nd and also the 24th president.

**6** Encourage students to try to make useful conclusions. For example, the statement, *All of the presidents were over 35*, is not very useful.

**8** Students may need to be reminded that Jamaal already recorded the first 10 presidents; they should begin with James Polk.

---

It is possible to organize the numbers into a new list or a diagram that makes it easier to see the distribution of the ages of the presidents at inauguration. This can be done in several ways.

4. **a.** Organize the numbers into a new list or a diagram that makes it easier to see the distribution of the ages of the presidents at inauguration.

   **b.** Write some conclusions that you can draw from the list or diagram that you made for part **a**.

Sarah made a **dot plot** of the presidents' ages at the time of their inauguration.

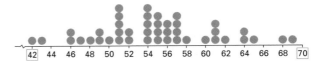

**Age at Inauguration**

5. **a.** What information is easier to see in this graph than in the list on pages 13 and 14?

   **b.** What information is missing?

6. Write at least three conclusions that you can draw from Sarah's dot plot. Write them in sentences beginning, for example:

   • Most presidents were about _____ at the time of their inauguration.

   • Very few presidents _____ .

   • _____ .

The value that occurs most often in a data set is called the **mode**.

7. What is the mode of the presidents' ages at inauguration?

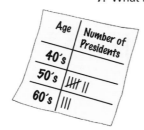

Jamaal thought it would be better to divide the ages into groups first and then look at what that might tell him. He made a table and tallied the ages of the first 10 presidents.

8. **a.** Copy Jamaal's table into your notebook and finish it. What does it tell you about the ages?

   **b.** Compare Jamaal's table to Sarah's graph.

---

## Assessment Pyramid

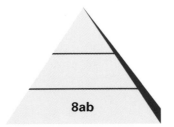

8ab

Collect, organize, and interpret data in tabular form.

## Reaching All Learners

### Vocabulary Building

*Mode*, the value that occurs most often in a data set, is defined on this page.

### Intervention

Students could be given a sheet with a number of possible sentences with only a few key words omitted for problem 6.

# Solutions and Samples

**4. a.** Answers and strategies may vary. Here is a sample strategy (a kind of tally chart).

| | |
|---|---|
| 42 | x |
| 43 | x |
| 44 | |
| 45 | |
| 46 | x x |
| 47 | x |

and so on. Examine students' strategies for attempts to order the data in some consistent way.

**b.** Answers will vary. Students may restate the facts from problems 2 and 3, or they may suggest new ones, such as that President Clinton was 46 when he was inaugurated, making him one of the younger presidents.

**5. a.** Answers will vary. Sample student response:

The graph is clearer than the list, since it is ordered. You can see at what ages presidents were and were not inaugurated.

**b.** Answers will vary, sample response. You cannot tell from the graph that the first seven presidents were all around 60 years old when they were inaugurated.

**6.** Answers will vary. Sample student's answers:

Most presidents were about 54.

Very few presidents were younger than 45.

Only one president was 69.

**7.** The mode is 51 and 54 years old. There were five presidents who were 51 and five who were 54.

**8. a.** A tally chart may look like the one below.

| Age | Number of Presidents |
|---|---|
| 40s | ЖЖ III |
| 50s | ЖЖ ЖЖ ЖЖ ЖЖ ЖЖ |
| 60s | ЖЖ ЖЖ |

The table tells, for example, that most of the presidents were in their 50s, and that there were more presidents in their 60s than in their 40s.

**b.** Answers will vary. Sample responses: Jamaal's table more clearly shows that most presidents were in their 50s when they were inaugurated. However, you cannot see how many presidents were exactly 57 years old at their inauguration. Sarah's graph shows these data.

# Hints and Comments

## Overview

Students continue exploring the U.S. presidents' data set. They organize the data set and make some statements about it. Students investigate a number line dot plot that represents the ages at inauguration, and they learn about the concept of the mode.

## About the Mathematics

There are several ways to organize the data. A number line plot and a tally sheet are on page 15 in the Student Book. Students should begin to understand that you lose some information when you go from numerical data to a graph (in the example above, the order of the ages at inauguration), but you also gain the ability to see other things (the cluster of ages from 54 to 58, the range, the two youngest ages, and the two oldest ages). There are three common one-number summaries of numerical data: the *mean* (see Section D), the *mode* (the value that occurs most often is introduced on this page), and the *median* (see Section E).

## Planning

Students may work on problems 4–6 in small groups. Problems 7 and 8 may be done individually. After problem 6, you may have a class discussion about problems 2–6, including the concept of the mode.

## Comments About the Solutions

**4. a.** Encourage students to organize the data using one of the graphical representations they remember from earlier units, such as number line plots or bar graphs. You might demonstrate how such data could be displayed more expediently using a graphing calculator or graphing computer software.

**8.** Jamaal's table is a frequency table, or a table in which the number of times each value (or group of values) occurs is counted. The frequency of a value is the number of times that it occurs.

# Stem-and-Leaf Plots and Histograms

## Notes

Stem-and-leaf plots are introduced on this page. In a stem-and-leaf plot, the tens and ones digits are separated so that all of the data is visible, but grouped.

Unfortunately, you cannot see the exact ages with Jamaal's method. One way to tally the ages so that you can see all of the numbers is to use a **stem-and-leaf plot**.

In a stem-and-leaf plot, each number is split into two parts, in this case a tens digit and a ones digit.

The first age in the list is 57. This would be written as:

| 5 | 7 |

You can make a stem-and-leaf plot like this one by going through the list of presidents on pages 13 and 14 and splitting each age into a tens digit and a ones digit.

**Presidents' Ages at Inauguration**

```
4 | 9 8 6 9 7 2
5 | 7 7 7 8 7 4 1 0 2 6 4 1 5 5 4 1 6 5 1 4 1
6 | 1 1 8 4 5
```
Key: 5 | 7 means 57 years

Note: So that everyone can read your diagram, you should always include a key like the one in the bottom corner, explaining what the numbers mean.

In the stem-and-leaf plot above, 4 | 9 8 6 9 7 2 stands for six presidents who were ages 49, 48, 46, 49, 47, and 42 at inauguration. All the ages at inauguration have been recorded except the last 11.

**9** Encourage students to work neatly and to place the ones digits in the stem-and-leaf plot directly under each other. This will help students to interpret the stem-and-leaf plot; they can compare the lengths of the leaves.

**9. a.** Copy and finish the stem-and-leaf plot. (You will start with Harry S. Truman.) Make sure you show the ages of all 43 presidents.

**b.** Compare this stem-and-leaf plot to Jamaal's table on page 15. How are they different?

**10. Reflect** Why do you think this diagram is called a stem-and-leaf plot?

Harry S. Truman
(1884–1972)

---

## Assessment Pyramid

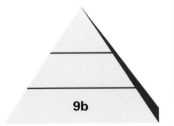

9b

Interpret data in tabular form.

## Reaching All Learners

### Intervention

Students can make their stem-and-leaf plot on graph paper to help make sure that it is as neat as possible.

### Extension

Students could create an additional stem-and-leaf plot. Possible data sources include: number of times students can jump rope in a minute, number of jumping jacks students can do in a minute, and students' arm length (in cm) from elbow to wrist.

# Solutions and Samples

**9. a.**

| Presidents' Ages at Inauguration |
|---|
| 4 ┃ 9 8 6 9 7 2 3 6 |
| 5 ┃ 7 7 7 8 7 4 1 0 2 6 4 1 5 5 4 1 6 5 1 4 1 5 6 2 4 |
| 6 ┃ 1 1 8 4 5 0 2 1 9 4 |

**Key:** 5 | 7 means 57 years

Students can quickly count the leaves to be sure that they have 43 presidents.

**b.** Answers may vary. Sample response:

The stem-and-leaf plot still shows all data separately, while Jamaal's table does not. You can count frequencies easily in both.

**10.** It is called a stem-and-leaf plot because the numbers with the higher place value form the stem (like the branch of a tree), and the numbers with the lower place value form the leaves. (See also About the Mathematics in the Hints and Comments column on this page.)

# Hints and Comments

## Materials

graph paper (optional)

## Overview

The stem-and-leaf plot is introduced. Students complete a stem-and-leaf plot.

## About the Mathematics

A frequency table is similar to a stem-and-leaf plot. A stem-and-leaf plot has a stem and leaves. The stem indicates the groups, and the leaves indicate how many values are in each group.

| | |
|---|---|
| S | l e a f |
| T | leaf |
| E | l e a f |
| M | l e a f |

In the example on Student Book page 16, the stem represents the tens digits, and the leaves represent the ones digits. A key that explains how to read and interpret the plot is very important.

## Planning

Discuss the stem-and-leaf plot. Explain why it is called that (problem 10), how to read it, and how it can be made. Also talk with your students about how you can find the mode in a stem-and-leaf plot. You may want to assign the Extension as homework. Students may work on problems 9 and 10 in small groups.

## Extension

You may ask students to make a stem-and-leaf plot for the data they collected on the heights of mothers and daughters. They should come up with a way of organizing their data that makes sense for the groups in the stem. This activity may be assigned as homework.

# Stem-and-Leaf Plots and Histograms

**Notes**

**11** Placing the ones digits in order makes it easier to read the data.

**12** The intent of this question is to get students to look more carefully at the stem-and-leaf plot data.

**13** You may want to encourage students to discuss which summary number that they know can best be used to describe the typical age.

You can make your stem-and-leaf plot easier to read.

**11.** Make two new stem-and-leaf plots to include the suggestions made above. (Be sure to include a key for each.)

  **a.** Make one plot that gives the ages in order.

  **b.** Make another plot that splits each row into two rows.

**12.** Consider your answer to problem 1 of this section for which you decided how old you thought a president of the United States should be. How many presidents were that age at inauguration?

**13.** What is the "typical" age of a U.S. president at inauguration? Explain your reasoning.

## Reaching All Learners

**Extension**

Students could be challenged to think of other ways to break up a stem-and-leaf plot into more than two groups per 10. This is difficult to do since 10 is only divisible by 5 and 2.

# Solutions and Samples

**11. a.**

```
4 | 2 3 6 6 7 8 9 9
5 | 0 1 1 1 1 1 2 2 4 4 4 4 4 5 5 5 5 5 6 6 6 7 7 7 7 8
6 | 0 1 1 1 2 4 4 5 8 9
```

**b.**

```
4 | 2 3
4 | 6 6 7 8 9 9
5 | 0 1 1 1 1 1 2 2 4 4 4 4 4
5 | 5 5 5 5 6 6 6 7 7 7 7 8
6 | 0 1 1 1 2 4 4
6 | 5 8 9
```

**12.** Answers will vary, depending on students' answers to problem 1 of this section.

**13.** Answers will vary. This unit has not yet introduced the terms *average,* or *mean.* Students may remember these terms from *Picturing Numbers,* however. Some students may say that 51 or 54 is the correct answer because it is the age that occurs most often. Others may say 55 because it seems to be in the middle. The mean is $2358 \div 43 = 54.84$ years.

# Hints and Comments

## Overview

Students manipulate the data in the stem-and-leaf plot from the previous page and think about typical numbers that describe a data set. The histogram is introduced.

## About the Mathematics

If the groups in the stems of a stem-and-leaf plot are too large, they can be split. This results in twice as many groups in the stem and makes the leaves shorter. A stem-and-leaf plot can easily be reorganized into a histogram (see problem 14a on page 18). A histogram is not the same as a bar graph. In a bar graph, the horizontal axis can have any type of categories (kinds of cars, sports, and so on). The bars can be arranged in any order. In a histogram, however, the horizontal axis is organized in sequential number intervals, such as 10–20, 21–30, and so on. The vertical axis in both a bar graph and a histogram indicates the frequency.

A data set can be summarized with one number. A one-number summary can be characterized as a typical value for the data set.

## Planning

Students may work on problems 11–13 in small groups.

# ◆ Stem-and-Leaf Plots and Histograms

## Notes

One way to manage the activity is to give each student a small post-it note and have him or her write his or her estimate on it. Students can then organize the post-its into a histogram on the board. It is easy to rearrange to try different sized bars, and this leads to a discussion that the next problem formalizes.

## Histograms

**Presidents' Ages at Inauguration**

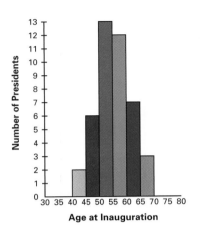

This graph is called a **histogram**. It is a histogram of the ages of the presidents of the United States at inauguration.

In this histogram, the ages have been put into groups spanning five years, so the width of each bar is 5 years. Ages 50 through 54, for example, are in the same group.

**14. a.** How can you use your stem-and-leaf plots from problem 11 to make this histogram?

**b.** Can you tell just by looking at the histogram how many presidents were 57 years old when they were inaugurated?

## Activity

### Your Teacher's Head

- Without measuring, estimate the length (in centimeters) of your teacher's head. Then collect the estimates from your classmates and make a histogram of the data. You will need to decide on a width for the bars.

- Now look at the collected data and decide whether to change your guess about the length of your teacher's head. When the class has agreed on a length, find out how close the real length is to the class guess.

## Reaching All Learners

### Act It Out

Students can use themselves to build a histogram of their guesses. Have the students decide on the groupings and then stand in line in the appropriate group.

### Hands-On Learning

Students could measure their own or a partner's head to help make an estimate.

### Vocabulary Building

A *histogram* is a graph that shows the distribution of a data set. The horizontal axis shows a numeric scale with intervals of the possible values, and the vertical scale represents the frequency.

# Solutions and Samples

**14. a.** A stem-and-leaf plot can be changed into a histogram by drawing a bar instead of writing the numbers themselves. Each number in the stem-and-leaf plot should make an equal contribution to the lengths of the bars on the histogram.

See the Hints and Comments column on this page for an illustration of how to convert a stem-and-leaf plot into a histogram.

**b.** No. When the numbers are grouped, individual numbers are lost. The histogram sacrifices specificity in favor of representing general patterns.

## Activity

Estimates will vary. A bar width of 1 cm would probably work well. Some students may have made a close guess while others may have been very far off.

# Hints and Comments

## Materials

graph paper (one sheet per student); measuring tape or ruler (one per group of students)

## Overview

Students do an activity to collect data and make a histogram.

## About the Mathematics

To make a histogram, data can first be tallied in a frequency table. A decision needs to be made about if and how the data are grouped. The frequency table can be made into a histogram.

## Planning

The activity may be done in small groups. Collecting all data is a whole class activity.

## Comments About the Solutions

**14.** Transforming stem-and-leaf plots to histograms may be seen as a two-step procedure:

**(1)** Box the numbers.

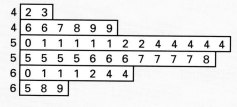

**(2)** Reorient the plot.

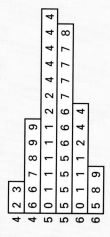

Note: The bar beginning at 40 includes all ages from 40 through 44. Each interval, or class, contains five values, for example, 45–49, 50–54, 55–59, 60–64, 65–69.

# C Stem-and-Leaf Plots and Histograms

## Notes

Before students look at page 19, ask them what makes the three histograms different.

Now look again at the Pearson and Lee data. Here you see three different histograms of the heights of the fathers.

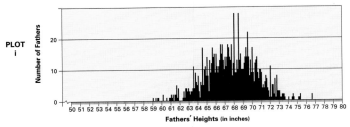

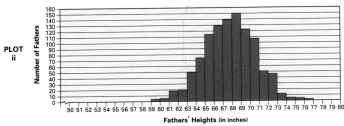

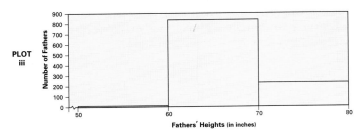

**15b** Note that this bar goes from 68 to 69 inches but does not include 69 inches.

Ask, *Why did the bar change vertically as well as horizontally?* (Because larger widths mean more data points in each bar.)

15. **a.** What is the width of a bar in each of the three graphs?

   **b.** On plot **ii**, which bar is the tallest, and what does that tell you?

   **c.** Write one conclusion you can draw from each of the plots **i, ii,** and **iii.**

   **d.** What happens to the information that is presented as the widths of the bars change?

16. Which of the three histograms gives you the most information? Say something about the heights of the fathers, using the histogram you chose.

## Assessment Pyramid

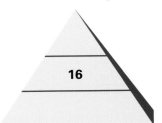

16

Compare different representations.

## Reaching All Learners

**Intervention**

If students have difficulty reading the graphs, have them look for the similarities and differences in the vertical and horizontal axes.

## Solutions and Samples

**15. a. Plot i**   The bar widths represent 0.1 inch.

 **Plot ii**   The bar widths represent 1 inch.

 **Plot iii**   The bar widths represent 10 inches.

**b.** There are about 150 fathers whose heights are between 68 and 69 inches.

**c.** Answers may vary. Sample student responses:

**Plot i**

No fathers are 76 inches tall. The most common height is between 68 and 69 inches.

**Plot ii**

There are more fathers that are between 69 and 70 inches tall than there are between 65 and 66 inches.

**Plot iii**

There are very few fathers' heights between 50 and 60 inches.

**d.** The greater the bar width, the less specific information the graph contains (as in plot iii). When bar widths become very small, however, the graph becomes more difficult to read (as in plot i).

**16.** Answers will vary. Each of the diagrams says something a little different.

The first histogram is the most detailed but says little about grouping. It is difficult to read the scale at the bottom (in tenths of an inch). A statement about it might be: There was no one height that occurred at least 30 times.

The second histogram is easy to read. A typical statement about it might be: There were about 100 fathers with heights from 59 to 64 inches.

The last histogram has bars that are really too wide to provide a useful summary. Statements about it might be: Almost all of the fathers had heights between 60 and 70 inches, and there were about four times as many fathers with a height between 60 and 70 inches as there were fathers with a height between 70 and 80 inches.

## Hints and Comments

### Materials

graph paper (one sheet per student); rulers or straightedges (one per student)

### Overview

Students revisit the Pearson and Lee data, and they investigate three histograms that illustrate how different interval widths affect the information displayed. Students analyze a histogram that shows the comparison of father-son heights. On the next page, they then make a stem-and-leaf plot and histogram using the mother-daughter height data from Section A. They write a paragraph about how mother-daughter heights compare.

### About the Mathematics

When the groups (or intervals) on the horizontal axis get larger, the scale on the vertical axis should be adjusted. When the width of the interval is increased, information is lost. A histogram can be used to compare data visually. For example two groups (fathers and sons) can be compared using one histogram. For reasons of clarity, one should not use too many groups when making comparisons using one histogram.

### Planning

Students may work on problems 15–17 in small groups. Problem 18 (on page 21) can be done individually.

# Stem-and-Leaf Plots and Histograms

**C**

## Notes

**17** This graph is easy to misinterpret. It is really two separate histograms that have been interlaced. Be careful that students do not make statements that indicate paring; in this graph, it is impossible to associate a father with his son.

In an attempt to compare the fathers' and sons' heights, Marcie made this graph.

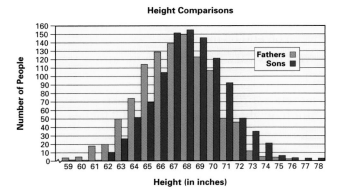

**Height Comparisons**

**17. a.** What does this graph tell you about the heights of fathers and sons?

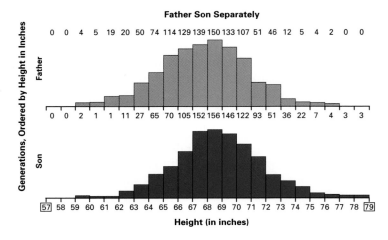

**Father Son Separately**

**b.** Do you prefer Marcie's combined graph or two separate graphs? Explain why.

**18.** Using the data you collected earlier, compare the heights of mothers and daughters using stem-and-leaf plots and histograms. Write a short paragraph about how the heights compare.

---

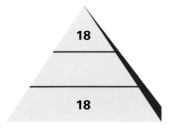
## Reaching All Learners

### Extension

After problem 17, ask, *How do the data displayed in the histogram here compare to the way the same data were displayed in the scatter plot you made in Section B?* (The data are not paired anymore. The father-son data sets are treated like two independent sets of data. In the scatter plot, the data are paired.)

### Intervention

You may need to break problem 18 into separate steps for some students or provide some of the graphs so that students can focus on interpretation.

## Solutions and Samples

**17. a.** There are more fathers than sons with heights of 66 inches or less; there are more sons than fathers with heights greater than 66 inches.

**b.** Different answers are possible. In the combined graph it is hard to see the actual position of the two "hills." The fathers' green hill is a little more to the left than the sons' blue hill, suggesting that the fathers were shorter in general. However, if the father's bars had been placed right of the sons' hills, the image would have been different.

In the two separate graphs, it is possible to properly see the slight difference between the positions of the two hills.

**18.** Answers will vary, depending on the data collected by the students. It is important that students refer to their data representations to justify their claims or conclusions.

## Hints and Comments

### Overview

Students make a stem-and-leaf plot and histogram using the mother-daughter height data from Section A. They write a paragraph about how mother-daughter heights compare.

### Comments About the Solutions

**18.** Students may make a histogram in any of the ways shown in this section. As students make different graphical representations, they should also see that different representations help them understand different features of the data—again, in both gaining and losing information.

### Writing Opportunity

You may have students write their response to problem 18 in their journals.

## Stem-and-Leaf Plots and Histograms

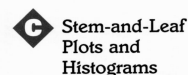

**Notes**

Challenge students to explain how the information in the graph supports Playfair's conclusion.

# Math History

### A Graph Can Tell More Than a 1000 Words Can

Anyone who listens to the radio, watches television, and reads books, newspapers, and magazines cannot help but be aware of statistics. Statistics is the science of collecting, analyzing, presenting, and interpreting data. Statistics appear in the claims of advertisers, in predictions of election results and opinion polls, in cost-of-living indexes, and in reports of business trends and cycles.

### A Graph

In statistics, graphical representation of data is very important. A graph can show patterns that are not visible in lists of data or tables. Can you imagine that graphs did not exist? Did you ever think of who invented certain types of graphs?

This is a very old graph. Do you know what this graph tells?

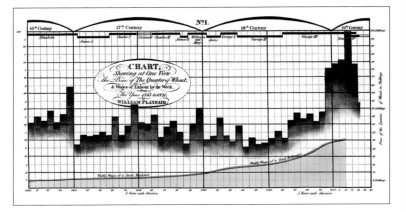

This graph was made by Scotsman William Playfair (1759-1823). William Playfair is said to be the man who "invented" three types of statistical graphs: the line graph, the bar graph, and the pie chart.

In this graph, Playfair compares the price of wheat to the average wage of a skilled laborer. He uses data of 250 years, from 1565 to 1821. Playfair concludes:

> ...that never at any former period was wheat so cheap, in proportion to mechanical labor, as it is at the present time.

---

## Reaching All Learners

**Parent Involvement**

This Math History may also be of interest to parents. Encourage students to share this information with their parents.

### Overview

Students review a historical note about William Playfair, the man who invented the line graph, bar graph, and pie chart.

## Notes

The Summary contains a number of terms that have been defined within the section. Be sure that students understand what each means.

### Summary

The **mode** is the data point that occurs most often.

**Stem-and-leaf plots**, **histograms**, and **dot plots** are different ways to represent data that make drawing conclusions easier. These graphs are based on reordering and grouping the data. With different graphs, you can see different things about the data.

Stem-and-leaf plots are typically made by hand to get a quick picture of the data.

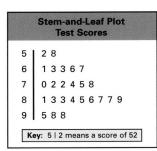

**Stem-and-Leaf Plot Test Scores**

```
5 | 2 8
6 | 1 3 3 6 7
7 | 0 2 2 4 5 8
8 | 1 3 3 4 5 6 7 7 9
9 | 5 8 8
```

Key: 5 | 2 means a score of 52

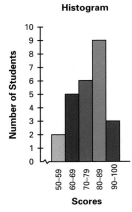

### Check Your Work

1. Anjinita's class measured the distance from their wrist to their elbow. She used a computer to make four different graphs. Which graph do you think she should use to display the class data? Explain how you made your choice.

**1** This problem is intended to make students think about when it is reasonable and useful to make a stem-and-leaf plot and when another type of graph makes more sense.

## Assessment Pyramid

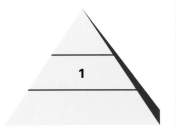

Assesses Section C Goals

## Reaching All Learners

**Parent Involvement**

Students can teach their parents the meaning of the terms in the Summary and show their parents the different kinds of graphs.

# Solutions and Samples

## Answers to Check Your Work

1. Your answers may vary. You may notice that histogram **a** does not give enough detail. You cannot tell, for example, how the lengths within the bar for lengths between 22–24 centimeters are distributed. The horizontal scale for histogram **a** also overlaps, so someone with a length of 22 centimeters could be in two bars. Either histogram **b** and **c** might be a good choice; they each have not too much detail but enough so you can see how the lengths are distributed. Histogram **d** shows too much detail. It is unlikely that someone would want to know the lengths in parts of centimeters (that is in millimeters). If the bar width gets smaller, each bar has less and less data, so histogram **d** is not telling you much.

# Hints and Comments

## Overview

Students read the Summary and do the Check your Work problems. They review the main mathematical concepts introduced in Section C.

## About the Mathematics

The mathematics in this section covers stem-and-leaf plots, histograms, and the mode.

## Planning

After students complete Section C, you may assign as homework appropriate activities from the Additional Practice section, located on Student Book page 48.

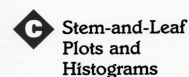

## Stem-and-Leaf Plots and Histograms

### Notes

You may want to point out to students that these four graphs all represent the same data set. The goal is not to find the correct graph of the data. Rather, the goal is to find which graph is the best for making sense of the data.

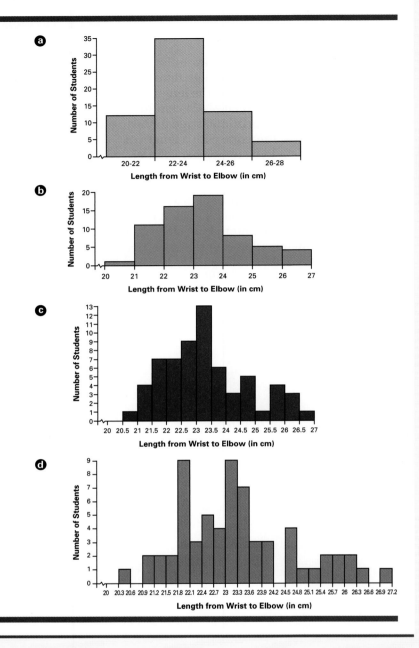

---

## Reaching All Learners

### Extension

This could be an interesting follow-up activity for your class. Have students measure and collect class data for the distance from wrist to elbow (in cm). Have each student group make a histogram of the data. Have students post their histograms and discuss the intervals each group decided to use to display the data. Have them compare their interval choices with the intervals used for the histograms on page 23.

## Hints and Comments

### Overview

Students read the Summary and do the Check Your Work problems. They review the main mathematical concepts introduced in Section C.

### About the Mathematics

The mathematics in this section covers stem-and-leaf plots, histograms, and the mode.

### Planning

After students complete Section C, you may assign for homework appropriate activities from the Additional Practice section, located on page 48 of the *Dealing with Data* Student Book.

## Notes

**3** This problem is intended to help students formalize their understanding about how different intervals change the appearance as well as the interpretation of a histogram.

Encourage students to use a set of data as an example so that they are able to refer to something while explaining the similarities and differences.

It is important that students realize that a scatter plot shows paired data and both histograms and stem-and-leaf show single variable data.

**For Further Reflection**

Reflective questions are meant to summarize important concepts from the section.

**2. a.** Someone proposes making stem-and-leaf plots of the Pearson and Lee data. What do you think of the idea?

**b.** Someone proposes making a stem-and-leaf plot of the ages of students in your class. What do you think of the idea?

**c.** A student suggests making a stem-and-leaf plot of the students' grades on the last test. What do you think of the idea?

**3. a.** List some of the advantages and disadvantages of a stem-and-leaf plot.

**b.** List some advantages and disadvantages of a histogram.

### For Further Reflection

One of your classmates has been absent for three days. Write several sentences that tell the differences among stem-and-leaf plots, scatter plots, and histograms. Include when it is best to use each type of graph.

## Assessment Pyramid

□ FFR

2, 3

Assesses Section C Goals

## Reaching All Learners

**Advanced Learners**

After problem 2, students could be challenged to use their lists to explain the similarities and differences between a stem-and-leaf and a histogram.

**Parent Involvement**

Students should share their work on For Further Reflection with their parents.

# Solutions and Samples

**2. a.** It is not a good idea. There are too many data points for a stem-and-leaf plot, because you usually make a stem-and-leaf plot by hand.

**b.** This is not a good idea either; the ages of students in your class will be pretty much the same, and so you would have only one or two stems.

**c.** This is a reasonable idea. There is some variation, and there are not too many data values.

**3. a.** Discuss your answers with a classmate. These are sample answers.

Advantages of a stem-and-leaf plot are that it can help you see the overall shape of the data, and it is easy to make one quickly.

Disadvantages of a stem-and-leaf plot are that if you have a lot of data points, they may pile up, and it will be hard to see any patterns or clusters. Some data sets do not have the right kind of numbers to make a stem-and-leaf plot easily (ones with very large and very small numbers, or ones with numbers that are very close together).

**b.** Discuss your answers with a classmate. These are sample answers.

Advantages of a histogram:

- You can use it for a large data set.
- You group the data using different bar widths to help you.
- You can see how the data are spread out and discover patterns.

Disadvantages of a histogram:

- You cannot see individual data points.
- You may not choose the appropriate width for the bars.

## For Further Reflection

For these data representations, students should point out that it is best to use stem-and-leaf plots when you want to see every numerical data point; histograms are best when you want to see groups of data; and scatter plots are best when you have two data sets that are related (like height and weight).

Answers will vary. Sample responses:

Advantages of stem-and-leaf plots:

- You can make one quickly by hand without a ruler.
- You can see every data point.

# Hints and Comments

## Overview

Students read the Summary and do the Check Your Work problems. They review the main mathematical concepts introduced in Section C.

## About the Mathematics

The mathematics in this section covers stem-and-leaf plots, histograms, and the mode.

## Planning

After students complete Section C, you may assign appropriate activities from the Additional Practice section, located on Student Book page 48.

Disadvantage of stem-and-leaf plots:

- It is difficult to make one with a large data set.

Advantages of histograms:

- You can make a histogram for a large data set.
- You can see the grouping of the data.

Disadvantages of histograms:

- You cannot see all of the data points.
- It takes time to determine an appropriate width (size of the interval) for each bar.

## Section Focus

Students learn to use the mean and the range to describe data sets. They explore different data sets. The mean is formally introduced in this section. Students learn how to find and calculate the mean and the range. They connect the mean to different types of graphs especially to histograms. Students also investigate situations in which the mean is not a meaningful statistic.

## Pacing and Planning

| Day 10: Hand Spans | | Student pages 25–27 |
|---|---|---|
| INTRODUCTION | Problem 1 | Discuss the typical hand span for a pianist. |
| ACTIVITY | Activity: Page 25 | Use a piece of string to estimate the average hand span of four or five students. |
| CLASSWORK | Problems 2–4 | Use the mean to describe the father-son and mother-daughter data. |
| HOMEWORK | Problem 5 | Use histograms to estimate the mean. |

| Day 11: Water | | Student pages 28 and 29 |
|---|---|---|
| INTRODUCTION | Problem 6 | Discuss typical water consumption for students in the class. |
| CLASSWORK | Problems 7–8d | Create a histogram of the water consumption data and use the mean to describe the data. |
| HOMEWORK | Problem 8e | Compare two data sets using the mean and the range. |

| Day 12: Sun and Snow | | Student pages 29–33 |
|---|---|---|
| INTRODUCTION | Problem 9 | Discuss the appropriateness of comparing the mean yearly temperature for two different cities. |
| CLASSWORK | Problems 10–12 | Investigate the advantages and disadvantages of using the mean to compare sets of data. |
| HOMEWORK | Check Your Work and For Further Reflection | Student self-assessment of Section D Goals |

| Day 13: Summary | | Student pages 30 and 31 |
|---|---|---|
| INTRODUCTION | Review homework | Review homework from Day 12. |
| ASSESSMENT | Quiz 2 | Assessment of Section C and D Goals |

Additional Resources: Additional Practice, Section D, Student Book pages 48 and 49

## Materials

### Student Resources

Quantities listed are per student.

- **Student Activity Sheet 3**

### Teachers Resources

No resources required

### Student Materials

Quantities listed are per student unless otherwise noted.

- Calculators
- String (4 or 5 pieces at least 30 cm long per group of students)
- Scissors

\* See Hints and Comments for optional materials.

## Learning Lines

### Using Statistics to Represent Data

In the unit *Picturing Numbers*, students were introduced to a compensation strategy for finding the mean. In this section, they should recognize that while compensation, or taking away and adding to values to make them equal, is adequate in finding the mean for a small data set, it is difficult to use that strategy to find the mean for 1,000 values. By the end of this section, students should be able to find the mean using the calculation rule or algorithm (adding the data values and dividing by the number of data points). The mean is not always a data point itself.

In addition, students learn to see that the mean by itself is not a sufficient way of comparing two groups because it says nothing about the spread of the data, and it can be distorted by extreme values, or outliers.

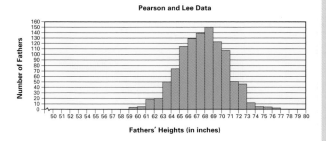

**Number of Bottles of Water Eighth Graders Drink Per Day**
1, 0, 0, 0, 1, 2, 3, 4, 2, 0, 1, 1, 0, 0, ⑬3, 2, 2, 0, 0, 1, ⑪ 1, 2, 3, 3, ⑬

In the context of mean yearly temperatures, students discover that the mean in itself does not tell much because the variation of the data is not reflected in the mean. In general, any single measure of central tendency will provide a weak description of a data set. A single number in combination with other numbers (range, minimum, maximum) and/or graphs gives a better picture.

### Representing Data in Graphs

In this section, histograms that were introduced in Section C are explored further. Students try to estimate the mean using a histogram of the data set.

**Pearson and Lee Data**

*Number of Fathers* (y-axis: 0, 10, 20, 30, 40, 50, 60, 70, 80, 90, 100, 110, 120, 130, 140, 150, 160)

**Fathers' Heights (in inches)** (x-axis: 50 51 52 53 54 55 56 57 58 59 60 61 62 63 64 65 66 67 68 69 70 71 72 73 74 75 76 77 78 79 80)

### At the End of This Section: Learning Outcomes

Students will:

- be able to find, calculate, and interpret the mean and the range of a data set;
- be able to estimate the mean from a histogram;
- develop a critical attitude toward using statistical methods to solve problems and make a decision; specifically they learn that the mean is not always a meaningful statistic;
- build an argument based on statistical measures, specifically the mean and the range; and
- solve problems by choosing appropriate statistical measures and graphs.

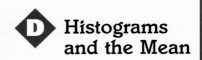 

# Histograms and the Mean

## Notes

This page reviews the concept of finding the mean using the compensation strategy introduced in *Picturing Numbers*. Some students may already know how to find the average by finding the sum and dividing, but encourage them to think in terms of compensation.

Students are more likely to use compensation if they are put in groups with an odd number of members for the activity.

**1c** You might want to suggest using a scale of $1:\frac{1}{2}$ so that the hand will fit on the paper widthwise.

## Hand Spans

For pianists, having large hand spans can make playing some pieces of music much easier. Hand span is the distance from the tip of the thumb to the tip of the little finger when the hand is extended.

Here are the hand spans of eleven pianists (in centimeters).

17, 21, 22, 19, 24, 19, 17, 19, 20, 21, 20

**1. a.** In what interval do the majority of these hand spans fit?

**b.** How does your hand span compare to the ones of the eleven pianists?

**c.** Draw a hand span to scale that you think is typical for a pianist.

Sergei Rachmaninoff (1873–1943), a Russian composer, had a very large hand span. He had a span of 12 white notes and could play a left-hand chord of C, E flat, G, C, and G.

### Activity

Use a long string to measure the hand spans of four or five students. Then use the string to estimate the average hand span. Be ready to explain to the class how you made your estimation.

22 cm    24 cm    17 cm    20 cm    17 cm

---

## Reaching All Learners

**English Language Learners**

The use of the term *typical* in problem 1c may be problematic for some students. Students could be asked to draw a hand that would represent the hands given.

**Extension**

Have students with access to a piano measure Rachmaninoff's hand span which reached across 12 white keys on the piano. Students can report their findings to the class. This activity may be assigned as homework.

# Solutions and Samples

1. **a.** The majority (7 out of 11 ) is between 19 and 21 cm. Some students may say the majority is between 19 and 22. This is also O.K.

   **b.** This answer depends on the size of student's hand. A student's hand span is probably smaller than the pianist's hand span.

   **c.** Answers will vary. Students may use a compensation strategy to find that 20 is the mean. They may also suggest drawing the mode, 19. The median, 20, may also be a possibility.

## Activity

Answers will vary. Students may measure the hand spans with one string "adding up," to estimate the mean, the string can be folded in 4 or 5 parts, the length of each part is the mean. If students use a separate string for each hand, the mean can be estimated by ordering the strings and using a visual compensation strategy.

# Hints and Comments

## Materials

pieces of string at least 30 cm long (4 or 5 per group of students); scissors (one pair per group of students)

## Overview

Students explore hand spans. They measure the hand spans of four or five students, then estimate the average hand span.

## About the Mathematics

The mean is introduced in the unit *Picturing Numbers*, using the notion of compensation. A compensation strategy takes away from higher values and gives to lower values until all are equal. For example, if students had test scores of 85, 75, and 80, five of the points can be taken from the 85 and added to the 75 to make all three scores equal. Then the mean is clearly seen to be 80. This section addresses other methods for finding the mean of a data set.

## Planning

Students may work on problem 1 and the activity in groups. The Extension may be assigned as homework.

## Comments About the Solutions

### 1. and Activity

One of the purposes of problem 1 and the activity is to review the concept of finding a mean by compensation and to set the stage for calculating the mean by finding a sum and dividing. Encourage different responses.

## Activity

Students should not be allowed to use rulers for this exercise. Be sure to have groups share their strategies. Later in the unit, students can use the data they collected here. To get a large data set, collect the hand span measurements from the entire class.

#  Histograms and the Mean

## Notes

This page formally introduces the mean.

**2c** In general, the mean (or median or mode) is not a reliable number by itself on which to draw conclusions. Some measure of how the data are spread out is also useful. This will be investigated later in this section.

**3** You can structure the discussion around the following data set: 2, 3, 3, 4, 5, and 19. The mean of the set is 6, which does not occur in the data set. This is also an interesting data set because the 19 is so much larger than the other numbers, that one number has a large effect on the mean.

## Fathers and Sons Revisited

Recall Tiwanda's statement from page 3: "I can say that the sons were generally taller than their fathers, because the total height of all of the fathers is 72,033 inches. The total height of all of the sons is 73,126 inches."

2. **a.** If you divide the fathers' total height equally over all 1,064 fathers, what would you estimate for the height of a father?

   This number is called the *mean height* of the fathers. The **mean** is one measure of the center of a list of numbers.

   **b.** Calculate the mean height of the sons.

   **c.** The mean height of the sons is larger than the mean height of the fathers. Is this information enough to conclude that sons are generally taller than their fathers?

   **d.** What other number(s) might you also give, with the mean, to help convince someone that the sons were generally taller than their fathers?

   Mai-Li calculated the mean height of the fathers correctly, but when she looked at the data set, she was surprised to see that only 18 fathers were exactly the mean height.

3. **a.** **Reflect** Are you also surprised by this fact? Explain why or why not.

   **b.** Does the mean seem to be a typical height in each case? Why or why not?

---

### Reaching All Learners

**Vocabulary Building**

The term *mean* is used on this page. The mean is one measure of central tendency of a data set and is calculated by dividing the sum of the data set by the number of values in the set.

**Extension**

Students could be asked to compare the compensation strategy (used in the hand span activity on page 25) for finding the mean with the strategy shown here. Students could be asked if the compensation strategy could be used to find the mean of the Pearson and Lee data. In fact, it could, but it would take far too long to balance 1,064 different heights.

# Solutions and Samples

**2. a.** 72,033 inches divided by 1,064 is 67.7 inches.

**b.** 73,125.7 inches divided by 1,064 is 68.7 inches.

**c.** Answers will vary. In general, the mean is enough information. However, it could be that there is a small group of very tall sons, while the other sons are only as tall as, or shorter than, their fathers.

**d.** Answers will vary. Sample response:

You can give the total heights of the sons and fathers, the highest and lowest height values for each group, or the spread between the high and low values in each data set.

**3. a.** Answers will vary. The mean doesn't split a data set in two parts with an equal number of data points (like the median does). The value of the data above and below the mean compensate each other.

**b.** Answers will vary. The mean does not have to be an actual data value. If the data have either many very high values or many very low values, then the mean alone will probably not be representative of the data, because the mean will be pulled up or down by those extreme values.

# Hints and Comments

## Materials

calculators (one per student)

## Overview

The mean and a calculation method for finding the mean are formally introduced, and the context of the heights of father-son pairs is revisited.

## About the Mathematics

The mean was introduced in the unit *Picturing Numbers*. The mean is a one-number summary for a data set. The mean by itself often is not very informative about the data set; it doesn't tell anything about how the data are spread out. The term *average* is also used for the mean. But technically the average can also be the mode or the median. Average is another word for a one-number summary of a data set.

## Planning

Students may work on problems 2 and 3 in small groups. The Extension activity can be assigned as homework.

## Comments About the Solutions

**3. b.** Students may wonder how the mean can be so different from any of the individual data. Remind them that a mean does not describe any individual data point but shows how the data balance overall.

# ◆ Histograms and the Mean

## Notes

This page helps students to see that the mean is the balance point for a histogram. If you think of cutting out a histogram and balancing it on a pencil, the pencil would be at the mean when the histogram balanced. This idea does not need to be formalized, but students begin to see it intuitively through these problems.

**4** This problem helps students get a feel for where the mean falls in a histogram. Students may be surprised that the mean does not have to be in the tallest bar.

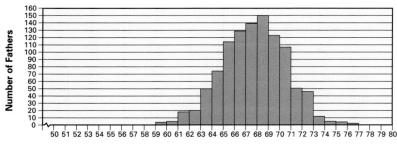

**Pearson and Lee Data**

Take a look again at a histogram of the heights of the fathers.

**4. a.** Between which two heights is the mean height located? (You found the mean in problem 2a.)

  **b.** Do the same for the histograms you made of the mothers' and daughters' heights for problem 18 on page 19.

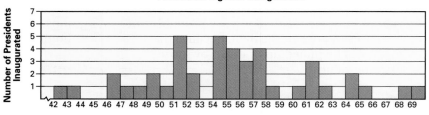

**Presidents' Ages at Inauguration**

Here is a histogram of the U.S. presidents' ages at the time of inauguration. Note: Grover Cleveland was counted twice because he was inaugurated twice.

**5. a.** Use the histogram to estimate the mean age at inauguration.

  **b.** Use the list on pages 13 and 14 to calculate the mean age at inauguration. Was your estimate close?

## Reaching All Learners

**Extension**

Students could be asked to create a histogram and estimate the mean for any of the data sets they have collected so far.

# Solutions and Samples

### 4. a.

**Pearson and Lee Data**

Fathers' Heights (in inches)

The mean is 67.7 inches (found in 2a.) it is located between 67 and 68 inches.

**b.** Answers will vary. Students should use their original data to find the mean, and then color the bar containing that mean on the histogram and name the two values that define the bar.

### 5. a. Estimates will vary. Estimates will probably be around 55.

**b.** The actual mean is $2{,}358/43 = 54.8$ years.

# Hints and Comments

## Materials

calculators (one per student)

## Overview

Students explore two histograms and use a histogram to estimate the mean. They check their estimate against the calculated mean.

## About the Mathematics

The compensation strategy can be used on the bars of the histogram to estimate the mean of the data. This can be accomplished by working toward the center from both ends, taking into account the marked intervals as well. If you do not take the empty unmarked intervals into consideration, you are using the median, or middle value, of the data set.

## Planning

Students may continue working in small groups on problems 4 and 5. The Extension may be assigned as homework.

## Comments About the Solutions

5. The estimates that students make will give you an opportunity to assess students' ability to find and interpret the mean of a data set.

# D Histograms and the Mean

## Notes

**6** This problem is intended to get students thinking about what reasonable numbers might be and about what kind of range is likely.

**7** Students may use a variety of strategies to find the mean. In particular, some students may group all of the zeros and multiply by their frequency, group all the ones and multiply by their frequency, and so on. This method is a precursor of methods used when working with grouped data, as is done later in the section. Some students who still use the compensation strategy should begin to see how other strategies may be more efficient.

## Water

Students at Fontana Middle School surveyed their classmates to find out approximately how many bottles of water students drink per day.

**6. a.** Approximately how many 12-ounce bottles of water do you drink per day?

**b.** Do you think this number is typical? Explain.

In a sixth-grade class, the students at Fontana Middle School found the following results.

| Number of Bottles of Water Sixth Graders Drink Per Day |
| --- |
| 0, 1, 5, 1, 0, 0, 5, 4, 5, 0, 4, 2, 1, 3, 3, 0, 1, 0, 4, 5, 5, 2, 4, 5 |

**7. a.** Find the mean number of bottles of water the students in this class drink per day. Show how you calculated the mean.

**b.** Do you think that the mean is a good way to describe the amount of water a sixth grader drinks per day? Why or why not?

## Assessment Pyramid

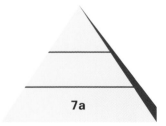

7a

Find and interpret the mean, median, mode, or range of a data set.

## Reaching All Learners

### Intervention

If students are only comfortable using the compensation strategy, give them a smaller data set that has the same mean. 0, 1, 4, 5, 1, 0, 2, 5, 4, 0, 3, 5 is a possible set.

### Extension

Students could be asked to come up with another list of numbers that has the same mean. Students will be asked to do something similar on page 30.

## Solutions and Samples

**6. a.** Answers will vary. Health agencies recommend that teenagers drink between 80 to 100 ounces of water per day.

**b.** Answers and explanations will vary. Some students may recognize that their daily intake of water often depends on the climate (for example, temperature and humidity), amount of physical activity, or the type of food they eat (for example, salty foods).

**7. a.** A total of 60 bottles divided by 24 students is equal to 2.5 bottles per person per day.

**b.** Answers will vary. Sample response:

The mean does not seem to represent most of the students, who either drank much more or much less than the mean.

## Hints and Comments

### Materials

calculators (one per student); graph paper (optional)

### Overview

The problems on Student Book pages 28 and 29 focus on representing and comparing data on the number of bottles of water that students drink per day.

### About the Mathematics

The mean can be found in several ways. The mean in itself is often not a reliable way to describe a data set because it gives no information about the spread of the data.

### Planning

Students may do problems 6 and 7 in small groups. The Extension activity may be assigned as homework.

### Extension

Have your class collect data on how many bottles of water each student drinks, and compare these data to the data on Student Book page 28. Students might collect these data in class, and they may work on organizing and interpreting the data set at home.

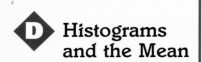

# Histograms and the Mean

## Notes

These problems help students discover that the mean alone is not a sufficient summary for a data set.

**8d** Students should recognize that even though the means of the two data sets are the same, the distributions might be very different. It is important to know something about the range and the shape of the distribution to understand the data more thoroughly.

---

Here are the results of the survey for an eighth-grade class.

| Number of Bottles of Water Eighth Graders Drink Per Day |
|---|
| 1, 0, 0, 0, 1, 2, 3, 4, 2, 0, 1, 1, 0, 0, 13, 3, 2, 2, 0, 0, 1, 11, 1, 2, 3, 3, 13 |

**8. a.** To get a picture of the data, make a histogram of the number of bottles of water the eighth graders drink per day. (Use another copy of **Student Activity Sheet 3**.)

**b.** How does water consumption for the eighth-grade class compare to that for the sixth-grade class?

**c.** Estimate the mean from the eighth-grade histogram and then calculate the mean from the data. How well did you estimate?

**d.** Would it be useful to compare the data for the two classes, using the mean? Why or why not?

Sometimes the mean is given together with the range. The **range** is the difference between the highest data point and the lowest data point.

**e.** Using the means and the ranges, write a few sentences comparing the number of bottles of water the sixth- and eighth-grade classes drink each day.

## Sun and Snow

San Francisco, California

Weather reports often give the average temperature for a city or region of the country. The mean yearly temperature in San Francisco, California, is 58° Fahrenheit (F), and the mean in Louisville, Kentucky, is 57°F.

**9. Reflect** Do you think using the mean yearly temperatures is a good way to compare the typical temperatures for the two cities? Why or why not?

---

## Assessment Pyramid

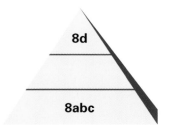

8d

8abc

Develop a critical attitude toward using statistical data.

Create and interpret histograms.

## Reaching All Learners

### Accommodation

Students could be given a piece of graph paper with the scales already marked to make the histogram.

### Intervention

In order to be able to compare the data on grades 6 and 8, students may need to make a histogram of the grade 6 data as well.

### Vocabulary Building

The *range* is introduced on this page. The range is the difference between the highest and lowest data points.

# Solutions and Samples

**8. a.**

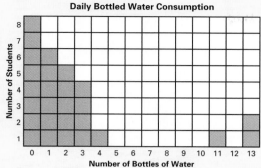

**Daily Bottled Water Consumption**

**b.** The histogram for the eighth grade is skewed. Most of the eighth-grade students drink very little water, but there are three students who drink very much.

The histogram for the sixth grade is symmetrical (the histogram's shape to the left and right sides of the mean are the same).

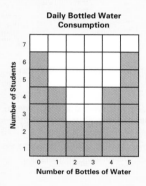

**Daily Bottled Water Consumption**

**c.** The mean is 2.5, the same as for the sixth grade. Students may estimate that the mean is lower, but because of the 4, 13, and 13, it is still 2.5.

**d.** The mean should not be used by itself. Because the means are the same, one might think that the eighth-grade class and the sixth-grade class drink the same number of bottles of water. But because the range for the second set is much bigger, this implies that some big numbers are raising the mean.

**e.** The mean for each class is 2.5 bottles of water, but the range of the sixth-grade class is 5 (0–5), while the range of the eighth-grade class is 13 (0–13). Students might say that the data on the eighth-grade class is more spread out than the data for the sixth-grade class, or that there may be a few really high data points pulling up the mean for the eighth-grade class.

**9.** Answers will vary. Students should point out, based on their work on water consumption, that the means can be the same, but the distributions may be very different. One city may have a much larger range or variation in temperature than the other.

# Hints and Comments

## Materials

**Student Activity Sheet 3** (one per student); calculators (one per student)

## Overview

Students continue analyzing the survey data regarding the number of bottles of water they now use in relation to these data from eighth-grade. The context of temperature is introduced. It is a very powerful one for developing mathematical concepts. (See also next page.)

## About the Mathematics

To compare two data sets about the same topic, two plots can be made and other characteristics of the data sets can also be used. These include the mean, the minimum (the lowest value), the maximum (the highest value), and the range or spread (the difference between the minimum and maximum values).

## Planning

Students may work on problem 8 in small groups. Problem 9 may be discussed with the whole class. This goes together with the problems on page 28 and 29. The Bringing Math Home activity may also be assigned as homework.

## Comments About the Solutions

**8. c.** Students should recognize that even though the means of two data sets are the same, the distributions may be very different. It is important to know something about the range and the shape of the distribution to understand the data more thoroughly.

**d. and e.**
The more measures (the mean, the range, a graph) are used to describe a data set, or to compare two data sets, the more accurate the description or comparison is.

**9.** Students may know that the temperature in San Francisco, California, varies less than the temperature in Louisville, Kentucky. This variation is not reflected in the mean, which is almost the same for both cities.

## Bringing Math Home

Have students survey their relatives and friends about the number of bottles of water they drink. Students can add these data to the data they have already collected and investigate how the mean changes.

# D Histograms and the Mean

## Notes

**10** If students are having difficulty getting started, ask them to give a possible list if they didn't know the range.

With a little encouragement, and a reminder about the compensation strategy, students may realize that having all of the mean monthly temperatures be 58 would work. From that point they may be able to make adjustments to account for the range given.

Louisville, Kentucky

In the table, you see the mean monthly temperatures for Louisville in degrees Fahrenheit.

| Month | Jan | Feb | Mar | Apr | May | Jun | Jul | Aug | Sept | Oct | Nov | Dec |
|-------|-----|-----|-----|-----|-----|-----|-----|-----|------|-----|-----|-----|
| °F | 33 | 38 | 47 | 56 | 66 | 74 | 78 | 77 | 70 | 59 | 48 | 38 |

The mean monthly temperatures in San Francisco range from 52°F to 64°F.

10. Make a table like the one shown above and write down what the mean monthly temperatures in San Francisco might be.

11. **a.** Based on all the information given, how do you think the temperatures in the two cities compare?

 **b.** **Reflect** Explain why it is important to know the range in addition to the mean.

## Assessment Pyramid

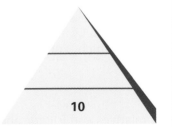

10

Collect, organize, and interpret data in tabular form.

## Reaching All Learners

### Advanced Learners

Students could be challenged to find two other cities that have very different climates but about the same mean yearly temperature. Almanacs or weather resources on the Internet can be used.

### Extension

Challenge students to come up with two sets of numbers that have the same mean but very different ranges.

# Solutions and Samples

10. Tables will vary. Students should compile a set of values that range from 52°F to 64°F and that have a mean of about 58°F. Some students may discover the important fact that the sum of the temperatures should be 12 × 58 = 696.

11. **a.** Answers will vary. The temperatures in San Francisco are much less variable than the temperatures in Louisville. Louisville is quite a bit hotter in the summer months and colder in the winter. Although they have almost the same mean, the temperatures in the two cities are quite different over the course of a year. The mean monthly temperatures for Louisville vary from 33°F to 78°F, for a range of 45°F. San Francisco has a smaller range (12°F) in its mean monthly temperatures.

    **b.** Answers will vary. Students may give examples of cities with a different range of temperatures but with means that are about the same.

# Hints and Comments

## Overview

Students compare the mean yearly temperature and the average monthly temperatures for two cities.

## About the Mathematics

The discussion of the mean associated with the range or spread of the data is continued. The mean can be the same for two data sets that differ in the spread of data.

The text on Student Book page 29 mentions the term *average*. This term is often used (in everyday language) to designate the mean. The average, however, does not need to be the same as the mean. The average is just another word for "a summary number" or "a typical number." You may want to make this issue explicit.

## Planning

Student Book pages 30 and 31 (and problem 9 on page 29) go together and can be taught in one class period. You may have students work on problems 10 and 11 in small groups.

## Comments About the Solutions

10. The actual mean monthly temperatures for San Francisco on which the given mean is based, are as follows: Jan 49°, Feb 52°, Mar 54°, Apr 56.2°, May 58.7°, June 61°, July 62.8°, Aug 63.6°, Sept 63.9°, Oct 61°, Nov 55°, and Dec 49.5°. The yearly mean and the monthly means vary slightly from year to year. On the Internet you can find actual weather data.

## Did You Know?

Two locations with identical latitudes may have different climates. One reason for this may be that they are different distances from the coasts. Water heats and cools more slowly than land does. In summer, bodies of water do not become as warm as the land, and in winter they do not become as cold. As a result, the inland area of a continent may be warmer in summer than the coast, which is cooled by the ocean air. In winter, the inland area of a continent may be colder than the coast, which is warmed by the ocean air. A large lake may have effects similar to those of the ocean on nearby land. The overall effect is that cities near major bodies of water experience less variation in temperature year-round than do those that are located some distance from major bodies of water. Thus, San Francisco, on the Pacific Ocean, experiences less year-round temperature variation than does Louisville.

# D Histograms and the Mean

**Notes**

**12a** Students can make an estimate of the amount of snow in their area in a typical year. If they are interested in finding the actual value, it may be available from an almanac or a local television or newspaper weather department.

**12d** This problem is intended to drive home the point that the mean is not always a useful tool in making generalizations about a situation.

According to a meteorologist, the mean annual snowfall in Boston, Massachusetts, is 42 inches. The meteorologist based his finding on records he made during the 10-year period from 1996 to 2005.

Boston, Massachusetts

12. **a.** Is 42 inches more than, less than, or about the same as the mean annual snowfall in the area in which you live?

 **b.** What does a mean of 42 inches tell you about the amount of snowfall in Boston over the years?

 **c.** Give an example of what the snowfall could have been each year from 1996 to 2005.

Russell says, "The mean snowfall per month in Boston was $\frac{42}{12}$, or $3\frac{1}{2}$, inches per month."

 **d. Reflect** What do you think about Russell's comment?

---

## Assessment Pyramid

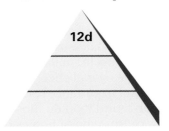

12d

Develop a critical attitude toward statistical methods.

## Reaching All Learners

**Extension**

Have students think of one situation where it makes sense to find the monthly average if you know the yearly average and one situation where it doesn't make sense.

**English Language Learners**

Students may not be familiar with the term *meteorologist*, a scientist who studies the weather.

# Solutions and Samples

**12. a.** Answers will vary. Student responses should be realistic, given historical local weather conditions.

   **b.** The total snowfall over 10 years was 420 inches.

   **c.** Answers will vary. Sample responses:

| 1996 | 35 | 42 |
|------|----|----|
| 1997 | 38 | 42 |
| 1998 | 44 | 42 |
| 1999 | 48 | 42 |
| 2000 | 49 | 42 |
| 2001 | 40 | 42 |
| 2002 | 37 | 42 |
| 2003 | 45 | 42 |
| 2004 | 41 | 42 |
| 2005 | 43 | 42 |

   Any answer is acceptable, as long as the total is 420 inches.

   **d.** Answers will vary. However, snow does not fall during every month of the year in Boston. Russell's calculation is technically correct, but it is misleading to imply that the snowfall is equally spread out over the entire year.

# Hints and Comments

## Overview

Students continue to explore weather data. On this page, they investigate mean annual snowfall.

## About the Mathematics

To get a good understanding of the mean, it is helpful to make a data set for a given mean. Doing so will reinforce the insight that there are many different data sets that might have the same mean.

## Planning

Students may continue working on problem 12 in small groups.

## Comments About the Solutions

**12. a.** Students might find this information on the Internet, in a local library, or in tourist information.

   **d.** This problem illustrates how the mean, by itself, is not always a useful tool to use in making generalizations about a situation.

## D Histograms and the Mean

### Notes

It is important that students read the Summary carefully and are clear on the use and meaning of the mean and the range. Students should understand that while the mean is frequently used, it is not always sufficient, or even useful, in summarizing a data set.

**1** Watching students work on this problem, or asking them to explain what they did, may give you a deeper understanding of how well they understand the mean.

**3** Students' stories will reveal their understanding of the different types of graphs.

**D** Histograms and the Mean

> **Summary** ⟩⟨
>
> The **mean** is the sum of the data values divided by the total number of values. The mean is a number that can be used to summarize the "center" of a group of data.
>
> An easy way to find the mean of a set of data is to add all of the numbers and divide by the number of data points.
>
> Often the mean is not even a data point. Sometimes the mean seems to be typical of the data points, and sometimes it does not. (Think of the example of the bottled water.)
>
> It is also important to know how the data are spread out. The difference between the lowest number of a set of data (the minimum) and the highest number of a set of data (the maximum) is called the **range**.
>
> The mean and the range together can be a useful way to describe data.

**Check Your Work** ⟩⟩

1. Find three numbers you can add to this data set that will not change the mean: 32, 10, 18, 33, 20, 37, 25.

2. Describe a situation in which the mean can give a wrong impression of a data set.

Here you see four different graphs.

3. Write a story that would match each of the graphs. Also name each type of graph.

a.

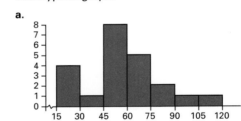

b.

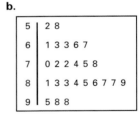

---

## Assessment Pyramid

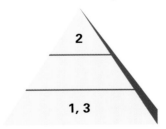

2

1, 3

Assesses Section D Goals

## Reaching All Learners

**Parent Involvement**

Students can share the Summary with their parents. Problems 2 and 3 are particularly well suited to students sharing their solutions with their parents.

# Solutions and Samples

## Answers to Check Your Work

1. Your answers may vary. The mean of the set of numbers is 25. If you choose any three numbers that average to 25, the overall mean will still be 25. So you might choose 26, 24, and 25, or 27, 23, and 25 or any other three numbers that work this way.

2. Many answers are possible. Discuss your answer with a classmate. Here is a possible answer.

   Suppose your grandfather takes his grandchildren for a trip. The age of your grandfather is 76. The ages of the grandchildren are 14, 10, 11, 8, 8, and 5. The mean would not give a very good representation of all of the ages.

3. The graph for problem 3a is a histogram. The graph for problem 3b is a stem-and-leaf plot. The graph for problem 3c is a dot plot. The graph for problem 3d is a scatter plot. Many stories are possible. For each of your four stories have a classmate read it to see if he or she thinks it is a good story for the data and the graph.

# Hints and Comments

## Overview

Students read the Summary and do the problems on these pages. They review the main mathematical concepts introduced in Section D.

## Planning

After students complete Section D, you may assign as homework appropriate activities from the Additional Practice section, located on Student Book pages 48 and 49.

**Notes**

**4** Hopefully students will realize that the stem-and-leaf plot and the dot plot can be converted to histograms by simply boxing the values.

**5** Be sure that students realize that some of the differences should be negative and some positive. This problem forces students to think deeply about what the mean really means. If students are struggling, have them think about how the compensation strategy works. In fact, the compensation strategy shows that the sum of all the differences should be zero.

**For Further Reflection**

Reflective questions are meant to summarize important concepts from the section.

c.

d.

**4.** Estimate the mean of the data in the stem-and-leaf plot, the histogram, and the dot plot shown in problem 3. Explain how you found each estimate.

In the newspaper Suli found the mean high temperature in her town last week was 72 degrees F. Also the mean high of each day was listed. She decided to explore how the temperature each day differed from the mean. When she added the differences, she got 0.

**5.** Did Suli make a mistake? Explain how you know if she was right.

### For Further Reflection

Think of at least two different ways of finding the mean. What are the advantages and disadvantages of each method?

**Assessment Pyramid**

FFR

5

4

Assesses Section D Goals

## Reaching All Learners

**Parent Involvement**

Students can work with their parents on making and explaining the graphs from this section. Parents may be able to share data and even graphs from their work or interests with their child.

# Solutions and Samples

**4.** The mean value for the dot plot and histogram is around 60. The mean of the stem-and-leaf plot is 78. If your answer for the mean value of the data in the stem-and-leaf plot is close to 77, you made a good estimate. You can make this estimation by looking at the plot and estimating where it "balances" overall, or you could estimate using the middle and frequency of each stem: 2 values at about 55; 5 values at about 65; and so on. You could use the same kind of estimation process for the histogram and the dot plot to get answers close to 60. For the stem-and-leaf plot, you could calculate the exact mean because you can see all data.

To estimate the mean values of the histogram and the dot plot you can use the same estimation strategies as for the stem-and-leaf plot, but you cannot calculate the exact mean since you do not have the exact values of all data points.

**5.** Suli did not make a mistake. You might think about the mean as "equal sharing" where if one person has 20 and the other 10, the first person gives the second 5 and they each then have 15. The first person loses 5 ($-5$) and the second person gains 5 ($+5$), so the sum of the differences is 0. Or think of the mean as the "center" of the data. The total amount they are worth is divided over the number of points. The total amount has to stay the same, so the gains and losses for all of the data points together have to equal zero.

## For Further Reflection

Answers will vary. Sample response:

You can find the mean by adding the data and dividing by the number of data points. You can also find the mean by using a compensation strategy, where you "balance" higher and lower numbers. When all of the data are "balanced," you have found the mean.

The compensation strategy is not very useful if you have a lot of numbers to work with or need a precise answer. Depending on the numbers in the data set, the advantage of the compensation strategy is that you might not need to do much computation.

# Hints and Comments

## Overview

Students review the main mathematical concepts introduced in Section D.

## Planning

After students complete Section D, you may assign for homework appropriate activities from the Additional Practice section, located on Student Book pages 48 and 49.

## Section Focus

Students use a number line dot plot to explore the growth of the United States. They investigate the median and quartiles and use these to create a box plot out of the number line dot plot. These plots show how data are clustered or spread out.

Students learn how to make and interpret box plots and how to find and use the median.

Students also use box plots to compare data sets; for example, they compare the heights of fathers to the heights of sons.

## Pacing and Planning

| Day 14: The United States | | Student pages 35–38 |
|---|---|---|
| INTRODUCTION | Problems 1 and 2 | Describe and diagram the growth of the number of states in the United States. |
| CLASSWORK | Problems 3–6 | Use the median and quartiles to divide a number line plot of the dates when each of the states joined the Union. |
| HOMEWORK | Problem 7 | Identify information in a box plot. |

| Day 15: Land Animals | | Student pages 39–41 |
|---|---|---|
| INTRODUCTION | Problem 8 | Introduce a new data set that lists the maximum speeds of various animals. |
| CLASSWORK | Problems 9–11 | Create and interpret a box plot of the animal speed data set. |
| HOMEWORK | Problems 12 and 13 | Compare two data sets using box plots. |

| Day 16: Back to Pearson and Lee | | Student pages 41–45 |
|---|---|---|
| INTRODUCTION | Problem 14 | Discuss the features of a box plot of the fathers' heights. |
| CLASSWORK | Problems 15 and 16 | Compare box plots of the fathers' and sons' heights. |
| HOMEWORK | Check Your Work and For Further Reflection | Student self-assessment of Section E Goals |

| INTRODUCTION | Review homework. | Review homework from Day 16 |
| REVIEW | Additional Practice or Section Summaries | Students review section or unit goals. |

Additional Resources: Additional Practice, Section E, Student Book page 49

## Materials

**Student Resources**

Quantities listed are per student.

• **Student Activity Sheet 4**

**Teachers Resources**

No resources required

**Student Materials**

No resources required

* See Hints and Comments for optional materials.

## Learning Lines

### Using Statistics to Represent Data

In this section, the median is formally introduced as the middle value of a data set. The median is a common statistic used to describe a data set using one number. The median in itself will not be enough to describe a data set in a meaningful way—information about the spread of the data is needed as well. In a data set, 50% of the values is above the median and 50% is below the median. The medians of each half of a data set are called quartiles. Students do not need to know this word, although they must be able to determine the middle values of the upper and lower half of a data set in order to be able to create a box plot.

### Representing Data in Graphs

The section begins with a number line plot of the dates of admission to the Union for all 50 states. The middle value (median) and middle value of each half (quartiles) can be found by dividing the data on the number line into four groups of equal size. Then a box plot can be made using the median, the quartiles, and the highest and lowest values.

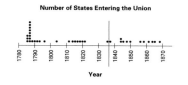

A box plot is a useful way to summarize a data set with only five numbers. The box (reaching from the 25th percentile to the 75th percentile) shows the distribution of the center (the middle 50%) of the data, and the whiskers show the spread of the first and last 25% of the data.

A box plot shows how data are clustered or spread out but does not show individual data points. Box plots are especially useful to compare the distribution of two or more large data sets.

### At the End of This Section: Learning Outcomes

Students will:

• be able to create and interpret box plots;

• find and interpret the median and quartiles of a data set;

• compare two data sets by using box plots;

• build an argument using the median, the spread, and box plots;

• develop a critical attitude toward using statistical methods to solve problems and make a decision; and

• solve problems by choosing appropriate statistical measures and graphs.

## Notes

This page and the next introduce the first context for this section.

You may wish to discuss the entry of your state into the Union. Then have students read the table on Student Book page 35. There are no problems for students to solve on this page.

# Box Plots and the Median

## The United States

A path from the parking area to Mount Rushmore National Monument in South Dakota displays the growth of the United States. The flags of all of the 50 states are along the path. A sign for each state shows the year that the state entered the Union.

## Reaching All Learners

### Accommodation

This would be a good opportunity to have maps of the United States available so students can locate the various states as they are discussed.

# Hints and Comments

## Overview

Students are introduced to the context of the first problems in this section: the years when different states entered the Union.

## Did You Know?

Texas, the 28th state admitted to the Union, has a complex and unusual history.

Originally charted in 1519 by Spanish explorers, the territory became an official province called "Tejas," which means "friends," in 1727. Since that time, it has endured arduous battles, and many countries—including France, Spain, Mexico, and the United States—have vied for ownership of the land. After a seven-month revolution that began in 1835, a special convention created an independent Texas republic. This republic lasted ten years, after which Texas joined the Union for a decade and a half. Texas then seceded to join the Confederacy. Years of reform—a period known as Reconstruction—eventually earned Texas readmission to the United States in 1870.

Over the past century, Texas has emerged as an impressively industrial and urban area. Today, Texas has one of the highest populations in the nation, proudly offers a first-rate public education system, and maintains notable contributions to the arts.

## Box Plots and the Median

### Notes

Have students spend some time looking at the table. They should look for times when a number of states joined the Union and periods where there was no growth. If students have studied American history, they can connect what they find to historical events.

This table shows the year of admission to the Union for each state.

| | | | | | | |
|---|---|---|---|---|---|---|
| 1. | Delaware | 1787 | | 26. | Michigan | 1837 |
| 2. | Pennsylvania | 1787 | | 27. | Florida | 1845 |
| 3. | New Jersey | 1787 | | 28. | Texas | 1845 |
| 4. | Georgia | 1788 | | 29. | Iowa | 1846 |
| 5. | Connecticut | 1788 | | 30. | Wisconsin | 1848 |
| 6. | Massachusetts | 1788 | | 31. | California | 1850 |
| 7. | Maryland | 1788 | | 32. | Minnesota | 1858 |
| 8. | South Carolina | 1788 | | 33. | Oregon | 1859 |
| 9. | New Hampshire | 1788 | | 34. | Kansas | 1861 |
| 10. | Virginia | 1788 | | 35. | West Virginia | 1863 |
| 11. | New York | 1788 | | 36. | Nevada | 1864 |
| 12. | North Carolina | 1789 | | 37. | Nebraska | 1867 |
| 13. | Rhode Island | 1790 | | 38. | Colorado | 1876 |
| 14. | Vermont | 1791 | | 39. | North Dakota | 1889 |
| 15. | Kentucky | 1792 | | 40. | South Dakota | 1889 |
| 16. | Tennessee | 1796 | | 41. | Montana | 1889 |
| 17. | Ohio | 1803 | | 42. | Washington | 1889 |
| 18. | Louisiana | 1812 | | 43. | Idaho | 1890 |
| 19. | Indiana | 1816 | | 44. | Wyoming | 1890 |
| 20. | Mississippi | 1817 | | 45. | Utah | 1896 |
| 21. | Illinois | 1818 | | 46. | Oklahoma | 1907 |
| 22. | Alabama | 1819 | | 47. | New Mexico | 1912 |
| 23. | Maine | 1820 | | 48. | Arizona | 1912 |
| 24. | Missouri | 1821 | | 49. | Alaska | 1959 |
| 25. | Arkansas | 1836 | | 50. | Hawaii | 1959 |

In 1787, Delaware became the first state. By 1959, there were 50 states in the United States. So the nation took 172 years to add all 50 states.

Jill says, "It looks like the growth of the United States was not steady. There were times when it grew quickly and times when it grew slowly."

1. Can you be more specific than Jill? Look at the list of states and write a few sentences in your own words to describe how the United States grew.

## Reaching All Learners

### English Language Learners

It may be helpful to read the names of the states aloud so that students become more familiar with the pronunciation of the state names.

### Parent Involvement

Students can ask their parents or grandparents about the history of the United States and whether they know why states entered the Union in this general order.

# Solutions and Samples

**1.** Answers will vary. Sample response:

In 1787 and 1788, many states joined the Union. Half the states had entered the Union by 1836 when the country was only 49 years old. The rest of the states entered over a period of 123 years, with a group of six states entering in 1889–90 and the last two entering in 1959. So the first half century of the United States saw faster growth in terms of the number of states than did the remaining years.

# Hints and Comments

### Overview

Students explore a table that contains information about when the states entered the Union.

### About the Mathematics

A picture, a graph, or a diagram often makes it easier to interpret information than a table showing all the data. The kind of graph or picture that one chooses depends on the information one wants to convey.

### Planning

Allow students to explore the table on Student Book page 35, looking for patterns, and then go on to work on the problems. The table on Student Book page 35 is used to answer problems 1–7 on Student Book pages 35 through 38.

### Did You Know?

Many states joined the Union in the aftermath of important historical events:

- Revolutionary War: Delaware, Pennsylvania, New Jersey, Georgia, Connecticut, Massachusetts, Maryland, South Carolina, New Hampshire, Virginia, New York, North Carolina, Rhode Island, Vermont, Kentucky, Tennessee

- Louisiana Purchase: Louisiana, Iowa, Mississippi, Illinois, Alabama, Maine, Missouri

- Gold Rush/Homestead Act period: California, Minnesota, Oregon, Kansas, West Virginia, Nevada, Nebraska, Colorado, North Dakota, South Dakota, Montana, Idaho, Wyoming, Utah

- World War II: Alaska, Hawaii

# E Box Plots and the Median

## Notes

This page begins the process of making a box plot.

**2** When there is an even number of values, the conventional method of finding the median is to find the mean of the two middle values. Introduce this idea after students have had a chance to talk about the possible solutions. One difficulty in this case is that the result would be 1836.5, which is not a way we usually express years. Since only the years of entrance and not the actual dates are given in this case, it makes the most sense to say something like *the median is some time in 1836.*

**3** This problem is intended to get students to notice that the median and the half-way point in the range are not the same. If the data were evenly spread over the range, they would be the same value.

A weekly magazine has organized a contest with the title "Write about the Growth of the United States." The rules state, "Often pictures tell more than words. You may use a picture or diagram to help people understand what you are saying."

Anita made the following dot plot of the data. (You can see the enlarged plot on **Student Activity Sheet 4**.)

**Number of States Entering the Union**

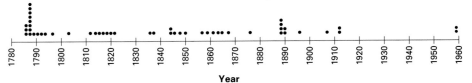

Year

**2. a.** By what year had half of the 50 states entered the United States?

   **b.** Draw a line to show your answer to part **a** on the dot plot on **Student Activity Sheet 4**.

The year that splits the group of 50 states into two groups of equal size is called the **median**.

Anita says, "I could use either 1836 or 1837 as the median of the group."

**3. a.** What does Anita mean?

   **b.** How would you choose a year for the median?

## Reaching All Learners

**Intervention**

Students could be asked to find the median of another data set. It is easier if the data are relatively spread out.

**Vocabulary Building**

The term *median* is introduced. The median is the middle value in a data set. The median can be found only if the data are ordered.

# Solutions and Samples

**2. a.** by the end of 1836

**b.**

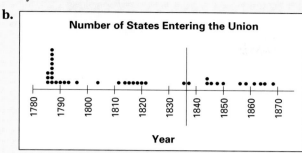

Number of States Entering the Union

Year

**3. a.** Since there are 50 states, dividing 50 in half yields two groups of 25 states. The years 1836 and 1837 are the two middle values.

**b.** Answers will vary. Statisticians have adopted the convention of taking the mean of the two middle values when there isn't a single middle value, that is, when there is an even number of values. This would be 1836.5.

# Hints and Comments

## Materials

**Student Activity Sheet 4** (one per student)

## Overview

Students plot the years when states entered the Union on a number line plot, and they learn about the median as another number that can summarize a set of data.

## About the Mathematics

A picture, a graph, or a diagram often makes it easier to interpret information than a table showing all the data. The median is the number whose value is bigger than half the numbers in a data set and is smaller than the other half. Students may know the word *median* from the context of "median of a highway," in which the median is the line between the two halves of the highway.

The median is also the 50th percentile, because 50% of the data have values below the median, and 50% have values above it. Just as the median is the 50th percentile, one can refer to other percentiles. The 25th percentile is the number that has a value greater than 25% of the numbers in a data set and smaller than the other 75% of the numbers in the set. The 25th percentile is also known as the first quartile, the 50th percentile (the median) is also called the second quartile, and the 75th percentile is known as the third quartile. Students do not need to know the terms *percentile* and *quartile*. However, they should understand the concept of quartiles.

## Planning

Students may work on problem 2 in small groups.

After they have finished this problem, you might have a brief class discussion in which you introduce the term *median*.

## Comments About the Solutions

**2. a.** If you are familiar with the history of how and when different states joined the Union (particularly your state), this would be a good time to introduce such information to your students.

**3.** It is important for students to agree to use the conventional method to find the median. Tell students that the median can only be found from ordered data.

# Box Plots and the Median

## Notes

**4** Students may have trouble understanding that the median of an odd number of data points is a point that belongs to neither half. The median of an even number of data points is the mean of the two middle numbers.

When discussing this problem, talk with the students about why the lines go through data points. This happens whenever the number of data points is not evenly divisible by four.

The median value is the value in the middle of a set of ordered numbers. If there is an even number of values, the median is the mean of the two middle values.

**4. a.** What year is halfway between 1787 and 1959? How does this year compare to the median year for the states?

   **b.** What does the median year tell you about the growth of the United States?

Note that the middle of the range is not the same as the median.

   **c. Reflect** Explain the difference between the middle of the range and the median.

To look more closely at how the United States grew, you can separate the states into four groups, each with an equal number of states. These groups are shown on the dot plot.

**Number of States Entering the Union**

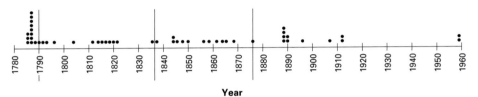

**Year**

**5. a.** Use **Student Activity Sheet 4** to verify that the states have been divided into four equal groups.

   **b.** What years divide the data into the four groups? Write them on the plot. Did a state enter the Union during any of those years?

   **c.** Once again, write a few lines about the growth of the United States. This time, use the dates you wrote on the plot to answer part **b.**

## Reaching All Learners

### Advanced Learners

Students could be asked to create a data set where the median and the middle value of the range are the same value. A further challenge is to create a set where the mean is also the same, or where the mean is different.

# Solutions and Samples

**4. a.** 1873. It is much later than the median year.

  **b.** The median year tells before what year the first 25 states entered the Union. Between 1787 and 1837, the first half of the states entered the Union. Between 1837 and 1959, the second half did.

  **c.** Answers will vary. Sample student answer:

Suppose you have data ranging from 1 to 10, let's say 1, 2, 5, 5, 5, 8, 8, 8, 8, 8, 9, 10, 10. The middle of the range is $\frac{1+10}{2} = 5\frac{1}{2}$. But the median is 8.

In the example of the states entering the Union, the middle value is 1873 and the median 1837. The middle of the range does not split the data set in two halves with 50% of the data in each half; the median does.

**5. a.** There are 12 states in each group. The vertical lines pass through two of the data points.

  **b.** The quartiles (the values that break the data into quarters) are 1790, 1836.5, and 1876. The middle quartile is equal to the median. Both the upper and lower quartiles are years when a state entered the Union: Colorado in 1876 and Rhode Island in 1790.

  **c.** Answers will vary. Sample student response:

The United States grew fast early and slower later on. By the year 1790, $\frac{1}{4}$ of the states had entered the Union, only three years after it was formed. By the year 1836, half of the states had entered the Union. So the Union was half grown in only 49 years. By 1876, the Union was $\frac{3}{4}$ grown in only 89 years. The last $\frac{1}{4}$ of the states came into the Union by 1959, an 83-year span.

# Hints and Comments

## Materials

**Student Activity Sheet 4** (one per student)

## Overview

Students compare the median with the middle value of the range. They continue their exploration of the years when different states entered the Union.

## About the Mathematics

The median is the middle value of all data. The middle of the range is a different kind of number. To find the middle of the range the frequencies of the data are not used. Students often confuse the median with the middle of the range.

The lower and upper quartiles are actually the median of each half. They are also the 25th and 75th percentiles, respectively. It is not important that students know the term *quartiles*, but you may introduce it if you wish. However, the concepts are important because they are used to make a box plot.

## Planning

Discuss problem 4c. (See About the Mathematics.)

## Comments About the Solutions

  **4. a.** One might say that the years that lie on the dividing lines belong to neither group, or that they belong equally to both groups. Here the convention used is that they belong to neither half.

  **b.** Students may have trouble understanding that the median of an odd number of data points is a point which belongs to neither half. The median of an even number of data points is the mean of the two middle points.

# E Box Plots and the Median

## Notes

This page formalizes the box plot from the lines drawn on the dot plot earlier.

**6a** Be sure students realize that "the box" refers to the entire box rather than one side or the other.

**6b** Be sure that students understand that the short whisker on the left indicates that one-fourth of the data are clustered, while the long whisker to the right shows that the last one-fourth are spread out over a wide range of years.

The dot plot can be turned into a type of graph called a **box plot**. A box plot is a graph that shows how the data are spread out.

**Number of States Entering the Union**

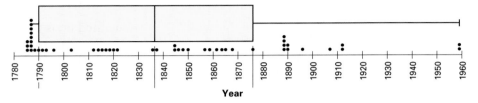

6. **a.** What was done to the dot plot to get the box plot? Where did the box come from?

   **b.** The line segments at either end of the box are sometimes called **whiskers**. How do you know how long to make the whiskers?

7. **a.** How many of the states are in the box? What fraction of all of the states is this?

   **b.** By which year had three-fourths of the states entered the United States?

   **c.** What does the box plot tell you about how the United States grew?

## Reaching All Learners

### Vocabulary Building

A *box plot* (sometimes called a *box and whisker plot*) is a graph that shows the distribution of the data by dividing the data in four groups with equal numbers of data points. The relative lengths of the four parts indicate the distribution of the data. The center section of the plot is the box, and the upper and lower portions are the whiskers.

### English Language Learners

Be sure students know what *whiskers* are, especially in terms of cats or dogs, because the term as used in the plot only makes sense if the term is known.

# Solutions and Samples

**6. a.** You make the ends of the box from the lines you drew dividing the data into four equal parts.

**b.** You draw the whiskers from the box to the first and last data points.

**7. a.** 25 states are in the box; this is one-half of the states.

**b.** By 1876, after 89 years.

**c.** Answers will vary. Sample response:

The plot shows that the first half of the states (those that entered the Union before 1836) entered the Union over a shorter time span than the last half of the states. The first one-fourth entered the Union in a very short time (three years), as indicated by the short segment on the left. The last one-fourth took longer (1876 to 1959, or 83 years) as indicated by the long segment on the right.

# Hints and Comments

## Overview

The box plot, a new way to display data graphically, is introduced.

## About the Mathematics

Box plots show the spread of data. They are based on five number summaries: the minimum, the first quartile (the middle of the lower half of the data), the median, the third quartile (the middle of the upper half of the data), and the maximum. The box represents the middle 50% of the data. Twenty-five percent of the data are represented by each whisker on the plot. Several box plots are often used to compare groups of data, especially when the data sets are large. However, individual data points are lost in such displays, and gaps and clusters cannot be detected.

## Comments About the Solutions

**7. c.** Students should always include a number line when making a box plot. Without it, the plot is just a "floating box."

# Box Plots and the Median

## Notes

**8** This problem is intended to get students to think some about the data before they begin making a graph.

**9** Be sure students understand that the data must be ordered to find the median and the quartiles.

**10b** Challenge students to come up with questions that could be answered by a different type of graph, but not a box plot.

**10c** The presence of two modes illustrates the difficulty of using the mode to summarize a set of data.

Variations in the box plots may be due to the fact that some students have ordered their data sets and others have not. Make sure the need to order data is addressed in the class discussion.

## Land Animals

| Animal | Speed (kph) |
|---|---|
| Bison | 50 |
| Cat (domestic) | 48 |
| Cheetah | 113 |
| Chicken | 15 |
| Coyote | 69 |
| Elephant | 40 |
| Elk | 73 |
| Giraffe | 52 |
| Gray Fox | 68 |
| Greyhound | 63 |
| Grizzly Bear | 48 |
| Human | 45 |
| Jackal | 56 |
| Lion | 81 |
| Mule Deer | 56 |
| Pig (domestic) | 18 |
| Pronghorn Antelope | 98 |
| Quarter Horse | 77 |
| Rabbit (domestic) | 56 |
| Squirrel | 19 |
| Warthog | 48 |
| Wildebeest | 81 |
| Wild Turkey | 24 |
| Zebra | 65 |

Animals run at very different speeds. A table of the maximum speeds of some animals is on the right.

**8. a.** How do you think these data were collected?

**b. Reflect** Write three sentences about the data in the table.

A box plot may help to summarize the distribution of the speeds of these animals.

To make a box plot, remember that you have to divide the speeds into four equal groups.

**9.** Make a box plot of the speeds of all of the animals. Use a number line and label your plot so that anyone can understand it.

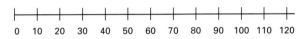

```
 |--+--+--+--+--+--+--+--+--+--+--+--+--|
 0  10 20 30 40 50 60 70 80 90 100 110 120
```

**10. a.** Use the information in your box plot to write two sentences that describe the speeds of animals.

**b.** Write a question about the speeds that cannot be answered with the box plot.

**c.** Write a question that can be answered easily with the box plot.

---

## Reaching All Learners

### Accommodation

Students could be asked to make a plot of only some of the data, or they could be given the plot already partially completed.

### Extension

Students could find additional animal speeds to make a new plot and observe how the plot changes as different animals are added.

# Solutions and Samples

**8. a.** Answers will vary. Sample response:

You could use a radar gun to measure their speed. To measure their maximum speed, you might have them chase fast prey or be chased by a predator.

**b.** Answers will vary. Sample student responses:

The cheetah is the fastest land animal at 113 kph.

The chicken is the slowest land animal at 15 kph.

The range is 15 to 113 kph.

Most speeds are between 40 kph and 81 kph.

The mean speed is 56.79 kph.

**9.** The quartiles are 46.5, 56 (the median), and 71.

**Speed of Land Animals
(in km per hour)**

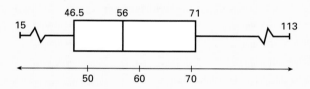

**10. a.** Answers will vary. Sample response:

The animals' speeds are between 15 kph and 113 kph. A quarter of the animals have maximum speeds of between 46.5 kph and 56 kph, and another quarter have maximum speeds of between 56 kph and 71 kph.

**b.** Answers will vary. Sample student responses:

What is the most common maximum speed?

How many animals have a maximum speed of less than 90 kph?

**c.** Answers will vary. Sample student responses:

Between what two speeds do 50% of the animals run?

All animals run between what two speeds?

# Hints and Comments

## Overview

Students are introduced to a new context, the maximum speeds of animals. They investigate the animal speed data and use box plots to describe the data.

## About the Mathematics

As with previous data sets that students have examined, it is important at first to describe the data in a qualitative way, using ordinary language. Before statistics are computed and graphs are constructed, it is helpful to get a feeling for the data by simply exploring the table for a while. On this and the next page, students investigate the purposes for which a box plot is a useful graph.

## Comments About the Solutions

**9.** Some students may have difficulty since this is the first problem in which they actually make a box plot. You might want to let students try to make the box plot without discussing the ordering and then have them compare box plots after they are done.

## Extension

You may want students to make box plots of the sets of data they collected earlier in this unit. You may want to assign some as homework.

## Did You Know?

Students may use the approximate formula 1 mile ≈ 1.6 kilometers, to convert the speed of each animal to miles per hour. For example, the fastest recorded speed for a human in a sprint is 100 meters in 10 seconds ≈ 36 km/hour; for a marathon, it is about 20 km/hour. Using the formula to convert these speeds to miles per hour: 36 kph is about 22 mi/h, and 20 kph is about 12 mi/h.

# E Box Plots and the Median

## Notes

**11** The intent of this problem is to get students to think about the possibilities before they begin. Challenge the students to sketch possible box plots before they look at the data.

**11b** Students should justify why they selected a particular plot. In answering part iii, students should use the speed data in connection with the animal, and not merely words such as fast and slow.

**12** Encourage students to make a stem-and-leaf plot to order the data.

Students may not be able to come to a definitive answer about which group is faster, but the box plots provide information and ideas for discussion.

A box plot can often help you answer some questions about data, but sometimes a box plot is not the best choice.

Suppose someone is interested in answering the following questions.

**i.** How fast does a human run (45 kph) compared to animals?

**ii.** What speed is most common for the animals listed on page 37?

**iii.** What clusters of data can be found? What does this tell you about the animals in each cluster?

**11. a.** How well would a box plot answer questions i–iii?

**b.** Answer each of the questions by plotting the data in a new way.

**c.** Using the plots you made in part **b**, what can you say about the mean, median, and mode for the animal speed data?

The animals have a wide range of speeds. In the tables on these two pages, the animals listed have been split into those with hooves and those without.

**12.** Do you expect to find a general difference in speed between the two groups? If so, what sort of difference do you expect?

| Animals without Hooves | Speed (kph) |
|---|---|
| Cat (domestic) | 48 |
| Cheetah | 113 |
| Chicken | 15 |
| Coyote | 69 |
| Elephant | 40 |
| Gray Fox | 68 |
| Greyhound | 63 |
| Grizzly Bear | 48 |
| Jackal | 56 |
| Lion | 81 |
| Rabbit (domestic) | 56 |
| Squirrel | 19 |
| Wild Turkey | 24 |

## Assessment Pyramid

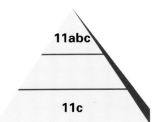

11abc

11c

Solve problems by choosing appropriate graphs.

Find and interpret the mean, median, and mode of a data set.

## Reaching All Learners

**Intervention**

For problem 11b, students could be asked to create the graphs from a smaller data set or could be asked to choose a plot from a collection of possibilities rather than creating their own.

**Extension**

Students could be challenged to characterize the clusters they identify in iii. *Where are the predators? Where are the prey? Do some of the slowest animals have other defense mechanisms?*

## Solutions and Samples

**11. a.** A box plot cannot answer parts i and ii. A box plot is only somewhat suited to answer a question like part iii about clusters of data. Stem-and-leaf plots or number line plots are more useful for these types of questions.

**b.** Here is a stem-and-leaf plot:

| | |
|---|---|
| 1 | 5 8 9 |
| 2 | 4 |
| 3 | |
| 4 | 0 5 8 8 8 |
| 5 | 0 2 6 6 6 |
| 6 | 3 5 8 9 |
| 7 | 3 7 |
| 8 | 1 1 |
| 9 | 8 |
| 10 | |
| 11 | 3 |

i. The speed of a human is below the median.

ii. Both 56 kph and 48 kph are modes.

iii. Three animals—the pig, the turkey, and the chicken—are slower than the rest of the animals in the list, with speeds equal to or less than 24 kph. They are easy prey! There is a large group of animals in the middle. The cheetah and antelope are very fast.

**c.** They are very close.

The mean is about 56.8 kph.

The median is 56 kph.

The modes are 56 kph and 48 kph.

The mean is the balance point between the speeds of the faster animals and the speeds of the slower animals.

The median divides the data into two equal halves in which half of the animals on the list run slower than the median speed and the other half run faster than the median speed.

The modes, 56 kph and 48 kph, are the recorded speeds that occur most often in the list.

**12.** Answers will vary. Students may suggest that animals with hooves will be faster than those without hooves, reasoning that hooves enable the animals to cover uneven terrain faster.

## Hints and Comments

### Overview

Students think about the purposes for which a box plot is useful.

### About the Mathematics

A box plot is useful to get a grasp of the distribution of the data (including the minimum, median, and maximum) and can be used to compare two data sets very well.

### Comments About the Solutions

**11. b.** Students might want to discuss or write that the slow animals are pigs and certain kinds of birds (some of which might be able to escape by flying). The fastest animals are large predators and herd animals (which are protected by their numbers). The animals in the middle speed range present a mixture of predators and prey, both large and small.

# E Box Plots and the Median

## Notes

| Animals with Hooves | Speed (kph) |
|---|---|
| Bison | 50 |
| Elk | 73 |
| Giraffe | 52 |
| Mule Deer | 56 |
| Pig (domestic) | 18 |
| Pronghorn Antelope | 98 |
| Quarter Horse | 77 |
| Warthog | 48 |
| Wildebeest | 81 |
| Zebra | 65 |

**13** Students can make a stem-and-leaf plot as a quick way to order the data.

**13a** Students can use the same number line as in problem 11, but you may want to let them discover this on their own.

**13. a.** Draw box plots for the animals with hooves and the animals without hooves. Put the two box plots above a single number line. (You will need to make your own number line.)

**b.** Compare the box plots. Does there seem to be any difference between the general speed of animals with hooves and that of animals without hooves?

**14.** Is it possible, based on this sample, to make a general statement about the speed of animals with and without hooves?

---

## Reaching All Learners

### Intervention

Interpreting and comparing box plots may be challenging for some students. If you have students share this work, you may be able to correct some of their misconceptions, such as that each whisker and half of the box plot should be of equal length because they all have $\frac{1}{4}$ of the data, or that hooved animals are slower because their box plot is smaller.

### Accommodation

You may want to prepare a transparency of the plots ahead of time, or have students make transparencies of their plots to share. You may also want to provide students with an appropriate number line.

## Solutions and Samples

**13. a.**

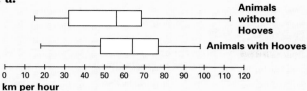

**b.** Answers will vary. Sample responses:

The animals with hooves seem to be faster than those without hooves.

The animals without hooves have a wider range and more variability, but all quartiles and the lower extreme are higher for those animals with hooves, indicating that animals with hooves might be considered faster (although the cheetah, which has no hooves, is the fastest).

**14.** No, you cannot make a general statement because you do not know how the sample was selected. Moreover, the sample is a bit small. Another sample could give quite a different impression.

## Hints and Comments

### Materials

transparency of plot of animals' speeds, optional (one per class)

### Overview

Students make two box plots to compare two sets of data.

### About the Mathematics

The power of box plots is illustrated when they are used to compare two sets of data.

### Comments About the Solutions

Note: Although students may or may not find a definitive answer to the question about which group of animals runs faster, the box plots provide information and ideas for discussion.

# Box Plots and the Median

## Notes

On this page, students connect two of the types of graphs studied, the histogram and the box plot. Notice that the scales on the histogram and box plot are about the same so that students can compare the graphs.

**15a** The wider the box plot (that is, the longer the whiskers), the more spread out the data.

**15b** Determining which graph is "better" depends on the questions to be answered. A histogram has all the data in it that are shown in a box plot, but a box plot gives a simpler picture and thus is often easier to read than a histogram.

## Back to Pearson and Lee

Here are a histogram and a box plot of the heights of fathers in the Pearson and Lee study. The data to create these graphs were obtained from **Appendix B**.

**15. a.** Explain why the whiskers of the box plot are relatively long compared to the length of the box.

**b. Reflect** Do you like the box plot or the histogram better? Why?

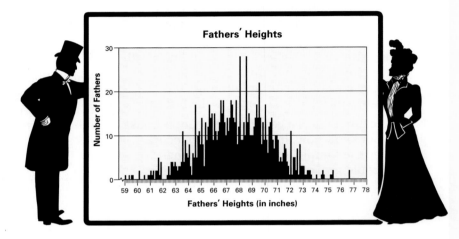

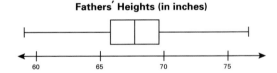

To compare the heights of fathers and sons, box plots can be used.

A box plot clearly shows the spread in heights. Placing the two plots one above the other makes comparing the heights of fathers and sons easy.

---

## Reaching All Learners

**Intervention**

If you copy page 40 onto an overhead transparency and then cut the two graphs apart, students can move the box plot directly over the histogram and see that the tall part of the histogram corresponds to the box in the box plot.

**Extension**

At this point, students have the tools to investigate a data-related question on their own. Students could either collect their own data, thinking carefully about their population and sample, or use data that has already been collected. There is a variety of sources of data both in the library and on the Internet.

# Solutions and Samples

**15. a.** This is because the heights of the smallest and largest 25% of the fathers are more spread out than the heights of the middle 50% of the fathers.

   **b.** Answers will vary. Sample responses:

The box is easier to draw, and you can see the distribution of the data at a glance.

The histogram is more detailed and gives a better picture of the distribution of data within a quartile. It also shows the shape of the distribution, whereas the box plot does not.

# Hints and Comments

## Materials

transparency of page 40, optional

## Overview

Students revisit the context of the Pearson and Lee data and explore the use of a box plot to describe the heights of the fathers.

## Extension Activity

Have students collect data about a topic and draw histograms, stem-and-leaf plots, and box plots to display their results and report to the class.

Possible topics might be the number of hours that students spend on the following activities:

- talking on the phone (per week);
- doing homework (per night);
- listening to music (per day);
- sleeping (per night);
- watching TV (per night or per week).

Have students work in pairs on a topic, then present their work to the class. This will afford them an opportunity to discuss whether they thought their sample was chosen in a proper way, which graphic display revealed the most information, and whether extreme values affected their results. Students will also find that they did not always use the right question. Their struggle with the data (Should time spent talking on the phone be recorded in hours or minutes?) will help them understand the need to clearly define their task before they begin to record data.

# Box Plots and the Median

## Notes

Spend some time having students look at the box plots before they begin the problems.

The data to create the sons' box plot were obtained from **Appendix C**.

Here are the two box plots.

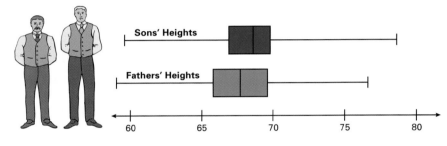

**16** Students should notice that the father's box is larger, that the father's left whisker goes farther to the left while the son's right whisker goes farther to the right. The median (line in the middle of the box) is higher for the sons.

**16a** You may need to help focus students on which aspects really support the statement and which aspects are true but are not helpful in supporting the statement.

**16. a.** How do the box plots support the statement that sons are generally taller than their fathers?

   **b.** What can you tell about the tallest 25% of the sons compared to the tallest 25% of the fathers?

   **c.** Write some other statements based on the box plots.

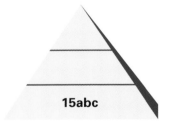
## Reaching All Learners

### Intervention

Provide students who are having difficulty with a copy of the box plots they can write on. Have them draw lines from the father to the son or vice versa so that they can clearly see where there are differences. Once they have done that, they can consider what each of the differences they discover means.

### Extension

Have students make box plots for the mother-daughter data they collected. They can compare the mothers to the daughters and also the present day data about women to the older data about men.

# Solutions and Samples

**16. a.** Answers will vary. Sample response:

- the median of the sons is greater than the median of the fathers;
- the tallest son is taller than the tallest father;
- the shortest son is taller than the shortest father;
- the box plot for the sons' heights lies farther to the right than the box plot for the fathers' heights.

**b.** The tallest 25% of sons are, in general, taller than the tallest 25% of fathers. Also, the heights of the tallest 25% of sons are more widely spread than those of the tallest 25% of fathers. (In other words, the line is longer.)

**c.** Answers will vary, but each of the various quartiles can be compared.

# Hints and Comments

## Materials

copy of page 43, optional

## Overview

Students use box plots to compare the fathers' and sons' heights.

## About the Mathematics

As in the animal speed problem, here is an example of the power of a box plot for comparing two data sets.

## Box Plots and the Median

**Notes**

The Summary for this section contains a great deal of information. Take the time to go over it carefully, emphasizing the median, dot plot, and box plot.

**Summary** ⟫

In Section D, you explored the mean. In this section, you explored the median, another number that can be used to describe the center of a set of data.

When you order an odd number of data points, the middle value is called the median. If there is an even number of data points, the median is the mean of the middle two values. The median value divides the data into two sets of equal size.

A dot plot can help you see the range of the data and how the data are clustered or spread out.

A box plot is another graph that shows how the data are spread out. To make a box plot, the data are ordered and then divided into four equal groups. A box plot shows how the data are distributed but does not show each individual data point.

**Number of States Entering the Union**

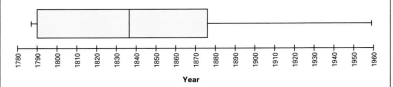

Five numbers describe the borders of the four groups in a box plot:

- the lowest number, or minimum
- the middle of the lower half
- the median
- the middle of the upper half
- the highest number, or maximum

Box plots are often used to compare different sets of the same kind of data, especially when the sets are large.

## Reaching All Learners

**Parent Involvement**

Students can go over the Summary with their parents. In addition, they could be given the five numbers for a particular data set and then work with their parents to create and interpret the box plot for that data.

**Act It Out**

It is possible to create a number line either on the board or the floor and then have five students position themselves as the five points on a box plot. They can then use string to show the box plot to the class.

## Hints and Comments

### Overview

Students read and review the main mathematical concepts introduced in Section E.

## Notes

**1** Give students a set of numbers to try this if they are unsure.

**2b** Remind students of the context in this problem. If you were riding in the car, or more importantly in the car in front of this car, what value would be most important for you to know?

## For Further Reflection

Establish criteria for evaluating students, such as:

- recognizing the problem and stating how these techniques help solve the problem;

- using both numerical and graphical procedures in their explanations;

- revising their first draft after initial teacher comments;

- presenting logical arguments and conclusions.

### Check Your Work

1. Jay claimed he could find the median by matching up the largest number and the smallest number, the next largest and the next smallest, and so on. What would you say to Jay?

The braking distance of one car traveling at 100 kph was measured 20 times. Here are the 20 braking distances with the values in meters:

57, 60, 52, 63, 58, 64, 68, 76, 54, 65, 61, 66, 80, 67, 53, 67, 65, 68, 70, 55

2. **a.** What is the median value of this data set?

   **b.** What number do you think would be most important in describing the braking distances?

3. **a.** List three things that you can learn about a set of data from a box plot.

   **b.** Give two ways in which box plots are useful.

4. Draw a box plot of data that are spread out evenly.

In this unit, data have been described using plots and numbers, such as the mode, the mean, the median, and the range.

5. Explain how you would use plots or numbers to do the following:

   **a.** See how the numbers in one data set are grouped.

   **b.** Compare two data sets.

### For Further Reflection

This unit has focused on dealing with data. You investigated the relationships between the heights of fathers and sons. Write two paragraphs describing what you learned about how to deal with data. Include how different techniques helped you in your investigations about the heights.

## Assessment Pyramid

1, 3, ◻FFR

2, 4

Assesses Section E Goals

## Reaching All Learners

### Intervention

For problem 4, if students are unsure, have them make a box plot for the data set 1, 2, 3, 4, 5, 6, 7, 8, 9, 10, 11, 12. Then ask them what they notice is different about that box plot from other box plots they have seen.

### Parent Involvement

Students can review their work with their parents so that they are sure that the ideas are solidified.

# Solutions and Samples

## Answers to Check Your Work

**1.** You can say different things to Jay. By pairing this way, you will eventually pair the two numbers on either side of the median—the last number and one that does not have a partner, or you will run out of numbers to pair. In that case, you find the mean of the last two numbers in your pairing. You may want to use examples to make clear what you mean. For example if the data are 3, 3, 4, 5, 6, 6, 6, 7, you match up like shown, so the median is 5.5.

**2. a.** The median is 64.5 m. This is the mean of the middle two values (64 and 65).

**b.** You may give different answers. Make sure you know the reason for an answer. For example, you can argue that the longest braking distance (80 meters) is the most important in describing the braking distances because this is the one to use to avoid accidents. Someone else may say that the most common distance (the mode) is the most important, because apparently this distance occurs the most. In this case there is not one number as a mode, 65, 67, and 68 each occur twice.

**3. a.** A box plot can help you see what numbers the middle 50% of the data is between, which interval has the lowest 25% or the highest 25% of the values, or the top half or three quarters of the values. The five values you can read from a box plot are:

- the lowest number, or minimum
- the median of the lower half
- the median
- the median of the upper half
- the highest number, or maximum

**b.** Your answers can vary. Here are some possible responses.

One way in which box plots can be useful is for comparing the spread and center of two or more data sets. Another way that box plots can be useful is to help you see how the data are spread out and where the center is in the distribution of the data.

**4.** If the data are spread evenly, the distances from the minimum to the box, from the left of the box to the median, from the median to the highest value of the box, and from this value to the maximum should all be about the same. See the following box plot.

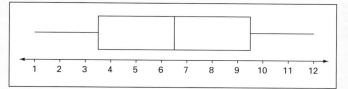

**5. a.** Plots: To look at one data set, you might use a stem-and-leaf plot, a histogram, or a dot plot to get an impression about the distribution of the data. A box plot might also work, although not as well.

Numbers: The mean, median, mode, or range could be used, although none would be as complete as a plot.

**b.** Plots: To compare two data sets, you could use box plots or scatter plots. A double histogram (one histogram on top of another) might also work, but it is not as easy to read. If the data are related in some way, you could use a scatter plot.

You can also make back-to-back stem-and-leaf plots if you have the right kind of numbers.

Numbers: The mean, median, mode, or range for each data set could be compared, although without the graph these may be misleading.

### For Further Reflection

Answers will vary. Students' responses should refer to the various ways they thought about the father-son and the mother-daughter data and how each method helped them make connections and understand relationships.

Students might go through the various plots and describe how each was useful in understanding the height relationships. For example, they might indicate that a stem-and-leaf plot might not be very useful for the father-son data because there was too much information, but histograms would be a good way to compare the distributions and still see the shape. If they used box plots, they could see how to make some comparison statements but they could no longer see any clusters or height groups. Students may do the same for the mean, mode, and median.

# Additional Practice

## Section A  Are People Getting Taller?

1. After studying the data from **Appendix A**, Sharon made the following statement:

   I can tell that sons grow to be taller than their fathers by looking at just the first 10 pairs of numbers. Within this set, 8 out of 10 sons are taller than their fathers.

   **a.** Why do you think Sharon looked at only the first 10 pairs of numbers?

   **b.** Is her statement convincing? Explain.

2. Describe how you might choose a set of fathers and sons that would help you explore the relationship between their heights without having to use all of the data in the Appendix.

3. Car company managers want to find out which new features car owners like best. What do you think of the information from the following samples?

   **a.** People looking at new cars at a new car lot on a Friday night

   **b.** Survey of all of the teachers in your school

   **c.** Survey of high school seniors who drive

   **d.** Telephone survey of people at numbers chosen by a computer in no particular order

## Section A. Are People Getting Taller?

**1. a.** Answers will vary, but Sharon probably thought that was the easiest way to get an impression of the set of data.

   **b.** No, the argument is not very convincing because there are many more pairs of numbers, and there is no reason that the first 10 pairs would be representative of the whole population.

**2.** Answers will vary. A systematic method is needed. The method must not prefer some data to be in the sample. One systematic method that works is to choose every 20th pair. The result of this sample is that 7 out of 10 fathers are taller.

**3.** Answers will vary. Possible student work:

   **a.** This is a good sample to get information from because these people are interested in new cars and are probably car owners.

   **b.** This is not a good sample to get information from. Not all teachers are car owners, and it may not be a good example of a group that is interested in new features.

   **c.** This may be a good sample, though high school seniors may not have the means to buy new features.

   **d.** If you contact people by telephone, you may reach a significant number of people who are not car buyers.

## Section **B** Scatter Plots

| School | Verbal | Math |
|---|---|---|
| Abraham Lincoln | 482 | 529 |
| Bravo | 443 | 496 |
| Columbus | 413 | 482 |
| Dewey | 426 | 472 |
| Eagle Heart | 413 | 482 |
| F. F. Johnson | 401 | 480 |
| G. Washington | 478 | 546 |
| Hardy & Laurel | 506 | 574 |
| Inter Urban | 474 | 523 |
| J. J. Forrester | 420 | 463 |
| K. Lopez | 426 | 475 |
| Lincoln Central | 434 | 477 |
| Madison | 417 | 518 |
| North | 456 | 513 |
| Ottey | 428 | 464 |
| Presley | 398 | 446 |
| Q. Waits | 461 | 508 |
| Robert Dail | 410 | 466 |
| South | 494 | 550 |
| Turner | 481 | 530 |
| United | 429 | 479 |
| V. Westward | 472 | 537 |

A school district has 22 high schools. At the end of the year, all seniors at these schools take a test with a verbal and a math component.

The mean verbal and math scores for each of the 22 schools are given in the table.

1. On a sheet of graph paper, make a scatter plot of the data. Label the horizontal axis "Mean Verbal Score" and the vertical axis "Mean Math Score."

2. **a.** What is the range for the mean verbal scores? For the mean math scores?

   **b.** The numbers along the axes for your plot should not start with zero. Why not?

3. Find the point that represents the highest mean verbal score. Does this point also represent the highest mean math score?

4. **a.** Find some points on your plot where the mean verbal score is equal to the mean math score. Draw a line through these points.

   **b.** What can you say about the scores of schools located above this line?

## Section B. Scatter Plots

**1.**

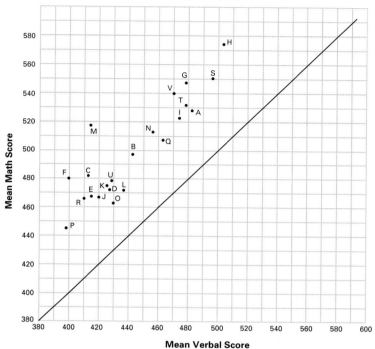

**Senior Test Scores**

**2. a.** The range for the mean verbal score is 108. The range for the mean math score is 128.

   **b.** If the numbers on the axes started with zero, that would leave a large part of the graph empty with all the scores crammed together.

**3.** The highest mean verbal score is 506, and that same school has a mean math score of 574. This is also the highest mean math score.

**4. a.** All points on the line drawn in the figure above.

   **b.** The schools located above the line have higher math scores than verbal scores.

**Additional Practice**

## Section C Stem-and-Leaf Plots and Histograms

Students in Mrs. Peterson's class competed in a long jump contest. The back-to-back stem-and-leaf plot below shows the results.

| Boys | | | | | | Girls | | | | | |
|---|---|---|---|---|---|---|---|---|---|---|---|
| | | | | **1** | 9 | | | | | |
| 9 | ? | 6 | 4 | **2** | 3 | 5 | 5 | 8 | 8 | |
| 7 6 6 2 | 2 | | | **3** | 0 | 1 | 4 | 4 | 6 | 7 |
| | | | 1 | **4** | | | | | | |

**Key:** 1 | 9 means 1.9 meters

1. How many students took part in the contest?

2. What number could replace the question mark?

3. What would the length of a "typical" long jump of the girls in Mrs. Peterson's class be? Explain how you found your answer.

4. Use the information of the stem-and-leaf plot to make a histogram of the girls' jumps.

5. Looking at your histogram, do you want to change your answer to problem 3? Why?

## Section D Histograms and the Mean

Mrs. Peterson's students also surveyed their grandparents to find out approximately how many hours of television they watched each day. The results are shown below.

| Number of Hours of Television Watched by Grandparents | | | | | | | | | |
|---|---|---|---|---|---|---|---|---|---|
| 2 | 3 | 8 | 5 | 4 | 3 | 4 | 9 | 4 | 9 |
| 3 | 4 | 8 | 10 | 5 | 2 | 3 | 1 | 9 | 2 |
| 8 | 3 | 9 | 3 | 2 | 4 | 4 | 3 | 2 | 5 |

1. Write three statements to describe the data set. If you rearranged the data or made a diagram, show your work.

## Section C. Stem-and-Leaf Plots and Histograms

1. 22 students

2. The question mark could be replaced by 6, 7, 8, or 9.

3. Answer may vary. Sample answer: About 3 meters. The jump of 1.9 m is an outlier and could be canceled out. The other data are clustered around 3.

4. Sample histogram.

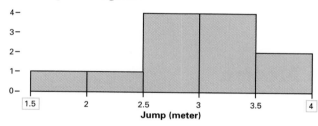

5. Answers will vary, depending on the answer given at question 3.

## Section D. Histograms and the Mean

1. Answers will vary. Students may have reordered the data and used tallies or made a histogram.

| Number of Hours | Number of Grandparents |
|---|---|
| 1 | 1 |
| 2 | 5 |
| 3 | 7 |
| 4 | 6 |
| 5 | 3 |
| 6 | 0 |
| 7 | 0 |
| 8 | 3 |
| 9 | 4 |
| 10 | 1 |

Sample answers:

• All grandparents surveyed watched television each day.

• Six and seven hours per day were not mentioned.

• Most people in the data set watch between two and four hours of television per day.

• There are two distinct groups: those who watch a lot of television and those who watch a relatively small number of hours.

• Three hours is mentioned most often.

2. Which better describes the typical number of hours the students' grandparents watch television each day, the mean or the mode? Why?

The mean yearly temperature for New York City is 55°F, and the mean monthly temperatures range from 32°F to 77°F.

3. Make a table showing what the mean monthly temperatures in New York City could be.

## Section E Box Plots and the Median

Different schools in the district entered a pumpkin-growing contest. Below are box plots of pumpkin weights from Carver Middle School and Edison Middle School.

**Pumpkin Contest**

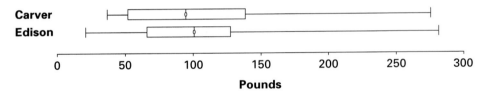

1. Which school had the heaviest pumpkin?

2. Daniel states that Carver has a better average (mean) weight, since the "box" of the box plot is larger. Do you agree with Daniel? Why or why not?

3. About how many pounds was the smallest pumpkin entered in the contest by Carver Middle School and Edison Middle School?

4. Which of the two schools has a larger range in weights?

5. The median for Edison is 102. Write a statement about the results of this school using the median.

6. A total of 24 students from Carver Middle School entered their pumpkins in the contest. The weights in the box of the box plot are between 52 and 140 pounds. About how many students had a pumpkin that weighed up to 52 pounds?

2. The mode is 3 (mentioned 7 times) but two or four hours are mentioned nearly as often. (The mean is about 4.7 but need not be calculated.) With this bimodal data, with two separate clumps, it is odd to use the mean as a typical value. Additionally, the data are too spread out to talk of the mean as a typical value. In this particular case, it makes more sense to use the mode, but in general the mode is not really a good measure of typicality.

3. Answers will vary since there are many temperatures possible, as long as the 12 temperatures add up to 660° and there is at least one 32° and one 77° temperature.

## Section E.  Box Plots and the Median

1. Edison won the contest because it entered the heaviest pumpkin of about 280 pounds.

2. Sample answer: I do not agree with Daniel. The size of the box only says something about the spread of the data, not about the position of the average weight (or the mean).

3. Edison: about 20 pounds, Carver: about 40 pounds.

   (Also accept the answer 20 pounds for both schools combined.)

4. Edison because it had both the lightest and the heaviest pumpkin.

5. Answers will vary. Sample answers:

   50% of the students had a pumpkin that weighed over 102 pounds.

   There need not have been a pumpkin of exactly 102 pounds. The two middle ones could, for example, weigh 100 and 104 pounds.

6. Six students because the whisker to the left of the box represents 25% of the data. Note that in theory the number could be less than six: if there happen to be a few data of exactly 52 pounds, there are fewer than six students with a pumpkin of less than 52 pounds.

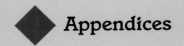

# Appendix A — Pearson and Lee's Data

## Heights of Fathers and Sons (in inches)

| Fathers–Sons | Fathers–Sons | Fathers–Sons | Fathers–Sons | Fathers–Sons | Fathers–Sons | Fathers–Sons | Fathers–Sons |
|---|---|---|---|---|---|---|---|
| 66.8–68.4 | 64.5–71.1 | 69.4–69.4 | 66.5–68.1 | 69.5–68.0 | 66.5–73.4 | 68.3–69.1 | 74.4–69.6 |
| 68.5–69.4 | 66.2–70.3 | 69.2–69.5 | 63.8–71.8 | 65.8–64.9 | 68.9–70.9 | 67.4–68.0 | 70.1–67.7 |
| 65.6–67.5 | 66.0–70.4 | 65.4–65.2 | 68.2–69.4 | 69.7–72.5 | 69.8–67.2 | 65.0–69.2 | 66.9–68.0 |
| 70.0–67.8 | 69.3–67.3 | 66.7–68.6 | 65.3–65.1 | 68.5–67.5 | 68.0–71.1 | 70.3–66.9 | 65.6–67.4 |
| 68.7–71.4 | 67.4–68.0 | 70.3–69.9 | 65.4–59.7 | 68.5–66.2 | 69.9–70.4 | 66.9–63.8 | 70.0–68.3 |
| 67.5–67.5 | 73.0–71.3 | 64.0–62.7 | 71.6–69.2 | 66.8–67.4 | 69.5–69.3 | 63.5–67.2 | 68.8–70.4 |
| 61.2–64.5 | 68.5–67.7 | 68.4–64.8 | 66.6–68.5 | 65.9–73.6 | 70.3–74.2 | 70.8–68.8 | 72.3–66.1 |
| 68.5–76.4 | 65.9–69.6 | 67.2–67.7 | 66.9–70.9 | 70.5–73.1 | 63.4–67.9 | 65.6–70.3 | 70.0–67.3 |
| 66.5–68.0 | 71.1–71.1 | 72.5–72.5 | 67.4–70.4 | 63.5–68.8 | 59.6–64.9 | 67.8–73.9 | 67.9–65.0 |
| 65.9–67.8 | 69.5–68.2 | 66.7–64.4 | 66.0–68.5 | 61.0–67.8 | 68.5–72.7 | 61.1–66.8 | 66.8–67.6 |
| 65.0–66.9 | 68.7–70.0 | 67.4–67.4 | 65.9–72.3 | 69.5–68.0 | 65.4–65.3 | 70.0–71.3 | 65.5–62.9 |
| 68.1–69.9 | 72.0–69.9 | 65.7–66.3 | 71.6–74.3 | 70.0–72.7 | 66.5–65.5 | 64.5–64.6 | 70.6–70.3 |
| 68.0–70.8 | 69.7–68.8 | 67.7–71.0 | 68.8–66.6 | 69.5–67.6 | 70.7–70.0 | 67.5–67.7 | 66.8–66.3 |
| 66.5–67.0 | 69.5–69.8 | 65.0–66.5 | 72.5–70.0 | 69.2–65.6 | 67.2–73.4 | 70.6–69.2 | 64.4–64.7 |
| 68.4–73.0 | 66.4–65.8 | 66.1–66.3 | 68.5–68.0 | 66.7–67.8 | 65.7–68.4 | 72.0–73.5 | 68.0–69.8 |
| 68.3–72.8 | 71.5–72.7 | 66.7–66.7 | 67.9–71.0 | 69.8–69.1 | 66.7–68.8 | 70.5–70.9 | 68.6–69.3 |
| 62.9–66.1 | 65.6–67.0 | 65.0–66.6 | 64.8–65.3 | 62.8–66.0 | 69.0–69.0 | 64.6–63.9 | 67.0–68.2 |
| 64.0–71.0 | 68.3–68.1 | 63.7–67.6 | 67.3–65.0 | 66.0–70.2 | 65.8–67.7 | 70.3–71.8 | 69.8–73.9 |
| 61.7–62.8 | 67.0–70.0 | 66.2–67.8 | 66.2–68.7 | 70.5–69.9 | 69.3–73.3 | 67.0–72.0 | 62.4–65.7 |
| 69.1–67.3 | 69.0–71.4 | 67.9–71.3 | 66.5–69.6 | 67.3–70.2 | 76.6–72.3 | 64.1–64.9 | 71.3–70.4 |
| 70.0–71.5 | 68.0–67.0 | 67.2–60.9 | 69.5–71.7 | 67.0–70.2 | 65.6–67.1 | 65.8–63.4 | 63.7–65.6 |
| 71.0–70.9 | 69.2–74.0 | 70.4–74.3 | 69.4–68.5 | 66.3–67.6 | 68.8–72.3 | 70.0–70.8 **400** | 62.7–64.7 |
| 68.0–67.8 | 69.4–71.8 | 67.3–65.7 | 70.0–71.8 | 67.1–66.3 | 65.5–67.3 | 63.9–64.9 | 63.2–67.4 |
| 66.0–64.3 | 64.9–70.9 | 66.3–69.7 | 68.5–71.5 | 71.0–68.4 | 67.5–68.0 | 65.0–67.5 | 67.7–68.2 |
| 70.6–72.4 | 61.8–63.9 | 64.4–69.2 | 71.7–69.7 | 68.0–67.1 | 67.1–68.0 | 65.3–65.3 | 66.0–69.3 |
| 64.7–66.8 | 67.6–71.4 | 60.1–66.5 | 70.9–68.7 | 69.2–69.5 | 69.2–70.3 **350** | 69.5–68.5 **350** | 70.9–63.6 |
| 67.9–71.1 | 63.7–65.0 | 66.6–65.5 | 67.4–70.0 | 65.5–65.0 | 72.2–67.8 | 66.5–67.0 | 68.7–70.4 |
| 67.3–71.1 | 68.3–71.3 | 66.6–67.7 | 67.3–67.1 | 65.7–63.9 | 65.7–64.9 | 68.4–67.6 | 65.3–63.7 |
| 70.3–68.5 | 65.3–63.9 | 70.7–70.9 | 64.5–65.8 | 68.4–73.6 | 64.8–65.4 | 66.9–68.3 | 69.7–69.2 |
| 65.6–63.5 | 68.5–68.3 | 64.5–71.4 | 69.5–63.6 | 68.0–77.4 **300** | 64.5–66.7 **300** | 65.0–66.7 | 67.6–67.4 |
| 65.3–67.5 | 68.9–71.2 | 69.6–71.8 | 69.4–70.0 | 67.3–68.6 | 68.2–67.0 | 68.3–67.9 | 70.2–70.7 |
| 64.6–69.5 | 68.4–67.8 | 65.3–63.4 | 68.6–70.5 | 65.4–67.5 | 62.5–67.1 | 65.5–71.0 | 69.8–70.3 |
| 70.7–70.3 | 67.3–68.3 | 67.6–66.9 | 67.2–66.7 | 65.8–66.4 | 69.5–66.9 | 67.2–70.0 | 63.4–67.7 |
| 67.3–67.7 | 67.6–70.5 | 71.5–69.8 | 69.2–69.6 | 64.0–68.6 | 67.1–68.8 | 70.1–68.6 | 65.4–71.7 |
| 67.9–67.2 | 68.0–69.7 | 66.6–65.6 | 69.5–68.6 | 71.4–68.4 **250** | 75.1–71.4 | 68.0–66.6 | 63.5–66.5 |
| 68.4–68.7 | 66.2–67.2 | 65.8–62.9 | 71.0–66.4 | 69.3–68.8 | 66.4–67.3 | 66.9–68.0 | 60.1–67.3 |
| 69.5–68.2 | 70.9–71.4 | 69.9–69.3 | 69.5–70.8 | 65.1–69.4 | 63.4–68.4 | 67.7–68.9 | 70.8–74.0 |
| 72.2–70.0 | 66.2–70.3 | 69.1–68.4 **200** | 66.5–64.7 **200** | 69.3–65.4 | 65.2–66.8 | 65.6–65.0 | 67.4–69.2 |
| 66.4–69.2 | 67.3–69.7 | 68.9–70.5 | 66.2–67.3 | 69.1–67.6 | 66.9–66.8 | 66.6–65.9 | 65.3–65.7 |
| 72.5–71.0 | 70.0–72.1 | 65.8–71.1 | 68.9–68.5 | 70.1–72.6 | 64.7–70.5 | 66.4–66.4 | 63.9–65.8 |
| 66.7–68.3 | 68.1–69.8 | 67.3–71.7 | 66.6–71.8 | 71.3–70.0 | 65.0–65.5 | 71.3–72.5 | 68.0–68.8 |
| 68.3–73.3 | 69.5–70.5 **150** | 67.7–70.6 **150** | 64.6–69.2 | 63.6–64.6 | 67.9–66.5 | 68.1–65.6 | 68.5–65.7 |
| 68.6–71.3 | 69.5–72.3 | 64.7–67.7 | 70.5–66.5 | 68.5–69.8 | 65.8–68.5 | 68.5–69.5 | 60.9–64.1 |
| 65.7–66.6 | 61.4–69.2 | 66.5–65.4 | 70.6–71.2 | 70.3–70.6 | 62.7–64.5 | 63.5–66.9 | 70.9–73.3 |
| 70.4–73.3 | 72.4–68.3 | 68.7–67.7 | 66.3–69.5 | 67.3–67.0 | 71.6–72.8 | 67.6–70.6 | 67.4–66.8 |
| 68.8–70.4 **100** | 67.6–72.8 **100** | 72.1–70.5 | 64.0–66.5 | 70.5–69.7 | 71.5–73.6 | 65.9–70.4 | 70.7–69.1 |
| 65.9–69.3 | 64.9–73.6 | 70.0–72.3 | 64.1–65.6 | 66.1–66.0 | 71.5–70.0 | 68.5–68.0 | 68.1–67.2 |
| 70.6–71.1 | 68.6–68.8 | 73.1–74.3 | 63.2–70.0 | 63.5–67.9 | 69.6–70.8 | 69.1–75.2 | 67.5–68.2 |
| 67.8–73.5 | 66.5–66.7 | 70.4–68.3 | 64.9–67.3 | 65.5–68.0 | 70.6–66.9 | 72.9–71.0 | 65.6–66.4 |
| 71.2–71.0 **50** | 63.5–66.3 | 68.5–70.2 | 67.8–67.8 | 65.5–67.0 | 69.5–67.8 | 71.6–71.2 | 67.9–74.9 |
| 72.7–77.5 | 65.6–73.6 | 69.5–69.2 | 64.9–64.8 | 69.3–69.3 | 61.8–66.6 | 69.0–69.1 | 67.2–70.9 |
| 66.7–64.4 | 65.8–71.0 | 71.6–71.4 | 67.9–69.5 | 68.0–66.5 | 65.7–67.9 | 72.0–72.2 | 70.7–70.4 |
| 65.6–64.3 | 73.4–68.9 | 67.2–66.2 | 63.7–70.5 | 65.9–66.3 | 71.9–72.0 | 63.7–68.5 | 71.4–75.1 |
| 67.7–68.9 | 66.9–66.0 | 69.2–70.5 | 68.4–69.0 | 70.4–66.9 | 74.5–74.2 | 71.1–68.0 | 73.3–73.4 |

# Appendix A — Pearson and Lee's Data

## Heights of Fathers and Sons (in inches)

### Panel 1

| Fathers | Sons |
|---|---|
| 69.8 | 70.6 |
| 69.6 | 70.2 |
| 69.0 | 70.4 |
| 66.4 | 64.4 |
| 69.0 | 71.7 |
| 65.6 | 63.4 |
| 63.0 | 64.2 |
| 63.0 | 69.0 |
| 73.5 | 71.1 |
| 68.0 | 68.3 |
| 72.0 | 72.0 |
| 65.5 | 65.8 |
| 68.0 | 70.9 |
| 69.6 | 69.4 |
| 66.9 | 68.9 |
| 70.9 | 70.0 |
| 64.7 | 69.0 |
| 75.3 | 70.5 (450) |
| 67.5 | 65.8 |
| 73.0 | 75.7 |
| 66.0 | 69.2 |
| 62.6 | 67.9 |
| 68.7 | 68.3 |
| 71.4 | 67.7 |
| 72.7 | 73.4 |
| 67.2 | 67.5 |
| 69.4 | 69.3 |
| 67.7 | 69.6 |
| 69.0 | 69.5 |
| 64.2 | 69.5 |
| 64.5 | 64.3 |
| 66.7 | 67.0 |
| 66.1 | 69.9 |
| 65.1 | 66.0 |
| 69.3 | 68.5 |
| 67.7 | 67.1 |
| 62.6 | 59.9 |
| 63.3 | 62.5 |
| 68.7 | 72.4 |
| 63.8 | 68.8 |
| 65.8 | 69.3 |
| 70.5 | 67.6 |
| 67.8 | 68.8 |
| 65.5 | 64.7 |
| 64.5 | 67.3 |
| 63.5 | 66.4 |
| 69.3 | 71.3 |
| 70.8 | 72.9 |
| 69.7 | 70.8 |
| 72.0 | 71.5 |
| 66.6 | 69.0 |
| 68.3 | 70.6 |
| 70.0 | 76.6 |
| 71.0 | 74.0 |

### Panel 2

| Fathers | Sons |
|---|---|
| 67.1 | 70.8 |
| 64.8 | 65.4 |
| 69.5 | 70.9 |
| 66.0 | 67.4 |
| 71.0 | 69.4 |
| 65.3 | 66.6 |
| 69.1 | 71.7 |
| 68.6 | 70.6 |
| 66.2 | 70.4 |
| 69.1 | 71.8 (550) |
| 64.6 | 65.0 |
| 63.7 | 69.4 |
| 64.3 | 67.5 |
| 68.6 | 69.2 |
| 65.7 | 67.8 (500) |
| 69.6 | 68.3 |
| 68.8 | 67.5 |
| 64.9 | 63.1 |
| 68.0 | 71.2 |
| 65.9 | 68.5 |
| 69.2 | 69.1 |
| 75.2 | 73.6 |
| 65.3 | 68.2 |
| 74.6 | 73.0 |
| 64.7 | 65.5 |
| 62.4 | 66.5 |
| 69.6 | 68.2 |
| 70.0 | 70.1 |
| 63.0 | 67.8 |
| 64.8 | 70.4 |
| 66.1 | 65.3 |
| 66.7 | 67.3 |
| 71.8 | 70.8 |
| 64.8 | 68.6 |
| 72.0 | 75.4 |
| 70.0 | 70.7 |
| 67.6 | 66.5 |
| 65.7 | 67.3 |
| 68.0 | 72.0 |
| 71.4 | 74.0 |
| 69.1 | 67.7 |
| 68.2 | 73.2 |
| 59.0 | 65.1 |
| 69.7 | 69.0 |
| 63.5 | 64.9 |
| 72.2 | 69.3 |
| 66.2 | 66.0 |
| 61.6 | 64.0 |
| 64.8 | 68.5 |
| 64.7 | 66.1 |
| 65.0 | 70.5 |
| 64.7 | 65.3 |
| 64.4 | 66.6 |

### Panel 3

| Fathers | Sons |
|---|---|
| 66.7 | 67.6 |
| 64.8 | 65.4 |
| 66.1 | 64.3 |
| 68.0 | 68.6 |
| 64.8 | 67.4 |
| 63.6 | 68.0 |
| 70.5 | 69.3 |
| 72.9 | 73.5 |
| 65.5 | 67.4 |
| 69.4 | 68.4 |
| 66.4 | 69.8 |
| 67.9 | 66.6 |
| 65.8 | 69.0 |
| 63.5 | 66.9 |
| 68.7 | 72.3 |
| 64.5 | 66.8 |
| 68.8 | 68.6 |
| 70.4 | 72.7 |
| 68.0 | 66.4 |
| 72.0 | 76.5 |
| 63.3 | 61.4 |
| 67.7 | 66.3 |
| 61.6 | 64.6 |
| 67.0 | 68.5 |
| 66.3 | 71.3 |
| 65.3 | 72.7 |
| 71.6 | 74.2 |
| 66.1 | 65.6 |
| 61.8 | 68.1 |
| 64.7 | 67.7 |
| 67.4 | 64.9 |
| 65.4 | 67.0 |
| 69.9 | 70.2 |
| 67.7 | 69.7 |
| 66.4 | 66.6 |
| 67.9 | 67.1 |
| 67.3 | 67.2 |
| 67.0 | 70.3 |
| 67.7 | 71.6 |
| 68.7 | 67.7 |
| 68.2 | 71.3 |
| 63.8 | 67.0 |
| 71.7 | 71.5 |
| 72.5 | 71.6 |
| 68.7 | 73.4 |
| 67.3 | 68.3 |
| 62.4 | 64.4 |
| 70.8 | 72.1 |
| 68.7 | 68.4 |
| 68.9 | 66.7 |
| 66.8 | 71.5 |
| 63.8 | 67.5 |
| 67.8 | 70.0 |
| 72.0 | 67.6 |

### Panel 4

| Fathers | Sons |
|---|---|
| 72.4 | 72.6 |
| 67.6 | 69.5 (650) |
| 70.6 | 71.7 |
| 65.1 | 74.5 |
| 68.5 | 71.4 |
| 70.2 | 67.2 (600) |
| 74.5 | 69.7 |
| 65.1 | 64.9 |
| 64.8 | 63.5 |
| 61.0 | 65.8 |
| 67.1 | 66.8 |
| 64.0 | 66.6 |
| 71.5 | 74.7 |
| 67.2 | 67.4 |
| 70.4 | 71.4 |
| 67.2 | 66.3 |
| 70.6 | 67.1 |
| 63.1 | 61.6 |
| 65.1 | 67.6 |
| 68.5 | 69.7 |
| 68.6 | 66.9 |
| 68.3 | 66.5 |
| 66.4 | 64.8 |
| 69.4 | 69.2 |
| 67.1 | 67.7 |
| 69.5 | 72.7 |
| 71.5 | 69.2 |
| 68.6 | 68.0 |
| 61.5 | 64.4 |
| 68.4 | 69.8 |
| 68.5 | 68.9 |
| 70.4 | 66.6 |
| 67.4 | 65.0 |
| 70.1 | 72.4 |
| 67.5 | 67.7 |
| 72.3 | 72.2 |
| 65.2 | 65.2 |
| 66.1 | 66.3 |
| 69.9 | 70.2 |
| 66.4 | 64.2 |
| 66.8 | 70.9 |
| 66.5 | 65.0 |
| 64.0 | 64.5 |
| 67.6 | 65.0 |
| 70.1 | 72.1 |
| 72.3 | 68.0 |
| 69.2 | 70.2 |
| 68.3 | 68.1 |
| 66.6 | 68.3 |
| 68.6 | 70.4 |
| 67.1 | 67.5 |
| 72.7 | 73.8 (700) |
| 69.3 | 69.0 |
| 67.8 | 63.5 |

### Panel 5

| Fathers | Sons |
|---|---|
| 65.6 | 68.6 |
| 66.3 | 68.0 |
| 69.0 | 70.3 |
| 70.8 | 71.8 |
| 66.4 | 68.2 |
| 61.4 | 72.0 |
| 68.1 | 72.6 |
| 70.9 | 69.8 |
| 65.0 | 63.8 |
| 68.7 | 70.1 |
| 68.0 | 69.2 |
| 60.8 | 67.7 |
| 69.6 | 70.9 |
| 67.4 | 66.6 |
| 64.0 | 67.8 |
| 69.0 | 71.2 |
| 69.1 | 67.1 |
| 65.3 | 68.7 |
| 73.3 | 78.6 |
| 69.7 | 69.9 |
| 62.6 | 68.8 |
| 72.5 | 68.0 |
| 65.6 | 67.7 |
| 64.3 | 65.0 |
| 68.4 | 69.6 |
| 65.0 | 66.8 |
| 60.5 | 62.0 |
| 71.4 | 69.8 |
| 67.7 | 69.3 |
| 66.3 | 69.8 |
| 65.3 | 71.2 |
| 65.2 | 64.5 |
| 64.7 | 65.9 |
| 68.0 | 69.1 |
| 68.4 | 67.5 |
| 65.4 | 63.5 |
| 69.3 | 69.7 |
| 70.2 | 69.4 |
| 69.2 | 68.2 |
| 71.7 | 68.0 |
| 68.8 | 68.1 |
| 63.8 | 64.4 |
| 67.3 | 71.5 |
| 66.9 | 68.1 |
| 65.3 | 72.2 |
| 69.6 | 69.4 |
| 72.2 | 71.6 |
| 66.2 | 64.4 (750) |
| 67.8 | 68.6 |
| 66.5 | 68.9 |
| 69.8 | 70.4 |
| 72.5 | 71.0 |
| 68.5 | 69.0 |
| 69.1 | 65.5 |

### Panel 6

| Fathers | Sons |
|---|---|
| 67.4 | 66.6 |
| 69.4 | 74.0 |
| 70.5 | 66.7 |
| 71.8 | 72.2 |
| 70.4 | 66.4 |
| 69.5 | 67.3 |
| 64.5 | 67.0 |
| 66.3 | 66.0 |
| 68.6 | 68.1 |
| 70.2 | 67.0 |
| 63.9 | 63.9 |
| 66.0 | 67.4 |
| 69.6 | 68.6 |
| 70.3 | 68.7 |
| 72.9 | 68.0 |
| 59.5 | 64.6 |
| 62.3 | 64.6 |
| 68.5 | 65.6 |
| 70.8 | 71.6 |
| 73.4 | 71.8 |
| 67.0 | 65.5 |
| 68.1 | 68.3 |
| 63.9 | 67.5 |
| 69.6 | 70.3 |
| 66.8 | 67.0 |
| 72.3 | 68.0 |
| 66.7 | 68.6 |
| 69.6 | 69.3 |
| 69.0 | 66.7 |
| 68.1 | 68.5 |
| 66.5 | 70.7 |
| 64.8 | 69.4 |
| 68.3 | 68.5 |
| 71.2 | 70.1 |
| 66.8 | 68.7 |
| 68.4 | 65.3 |
| 67.7 | 66.7 |
| 67.9 | 64.9 |
| 71.2 | 65.6 |
| 65.7 | 69.2 |
| 63.4 | 66.3 |
| 68.9 | 67.9 |
| 70.9 | 71.8 |
| 67.1 | 68.1 |
| 72.7 | 68.2 |
| 70.1 | 70.8 |
| 66.0 | 67.0 |
| 67.0 | 67.9 |
| 70.4 | 69.3 |
| 61.2 | 67.4 |
| 70.3 | 69.7 |
| 68.9 | 70.5 |
| 71.0 | 69.0 |
| 66.8 | 71.7 |

### Panel 7

| Fathers | Sons |
|---|---|
| 71.0 | 72.2 |
| 69.6 | 69.2 |
| 68.1 | 70.7 |
| 66.3 | 71.4 |
| 69.9 | 70.5 |
| 70.5 | 70.0 |
| 68.2 | 69.7 |
| 69.9 | 78.0 |
| 67.4 | 66.0 |
| 67.6 | 69.3 |
| 67.0 | 67.5 |
| 66.7 | 68.9 |
| 66.4 | 68.3 |
| 65.1 | 67.6 |
| 66.5 | 70.1 |
| 65.8 | 69.7 |
| 69.1 | 66.5 |
| 72.8 | 77.4 |
| 63.3 | 67.2 |
| 66.7 | 66.3 |
| 71.8 | 69.5 |
| 70.8 | 73.0 |
| 67.1 | 62.5 |
| 69.3 | 68.7 |
| 63.9 | 62.4 |
| 69.9 | 69.3 |
| 66.7 | 72.5 |
| 69.8 | 68.1 |
| 68.6 | 69.4 |
| 65.0 | 71.0 |
| 70.8 | 63.1 |
| 68.0 | 65.8 |
| 70.0 | 67.1 |
| 69.4 | 71.3 |
| 68.3 | 74.4 |
| 70.5 | 68.4 |
| 69.7 | 71.3 |
| 68.5 | 66.6 |
| 64.7 | 68.4 |
| 69.3 | 69.9 (850) |
| 65.9 | 65.7 |
| 72.0 | 68.6 |
| 66.6 | 62.8 |
| 66.8 | 69.5 (800) |
| 70.0 | 67.5 |
| 75.3 | 68.9 |
| 68.8 | 74.8 |
| 69.8 | 69.9 |
| 68.7 | 70.5 |
| 61.2 | 67.4 |
| 64.5 | 69.0 |
| 68.5 | 67.7 |
| 69.2 | 69.2 |
| 72.0 | 68.1 |
| 64.5 | 65.7 |

### Panel 8

| Fathers | Sons |
|---|---|
| 69.8 | 65.1 |
| 63.5 | 64.5 |
| 70.3 | 68.1 |
| 68.6 | 72.1 |
| 66.7 | 71.1 |
| 66.8 | 64.8 |
| 68.2 | 65.8 |
| 68.5 | 69.8 |
| 67.3 | 65.4 |
| 73.5 | 71.3 |
| 66.1 | 68.9 |
| 69.1 | 73.6 |
| 67.5 | 67.1 |
| 68.2 | 67.0 |
| 64.1 | 66.7 |
| 65.6 | 62.5 |
| 69.2 | 63.8 |
| 70.0 | 68.3 |
| 70.9 | 70.2 |
| 69.7 | 69.5 |
| 72.0 | 71.9 |
| 70.5 | 74.5 |
| 68.8 | 67.7 |
| 69.4 | 70.2 |
| 67.1 | 69.3 |
| 66.3 | 66.1 |
| 70.4 | 66.9 |
| 64.3 | 66.9 |
| 68.4 | 68.0 |
| 67.7 | 71.4 |
| 68.5 | 69.0 |
| 67.5 | 71.8 |
| 65.0 | 69.0 |
| 66.8 | 62.3 |
| 68.0 | 71.4 |
| 70.7 | 70.7 |
| 68.1 | 73.1 |
| 65.1 | 70.0 |
| 70.7 | 72.4 |
| 65.8 | 69.4 |
| 66.8 | 66.7 |
| 69.6 | 69.3 |
| 69.8 | 70.0 |
| 66.5 | 65.3 |
| 69.4 | 67.7 |
| 67.0 | 66.0 |
| 73.0 | 69.5 |
| 71.1 | 73.2 |
| 64.5 | 67.2 |
| 72.8 | 75.5 |
| 70.2 | 72.4 |
| 68.5 | 73.3 |
| 66.0 | 71.3 |
| 72.5 | 70.7 |

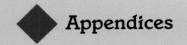

# Appendix A — Pearson and Lee's Data

## Heights of Fathers and Sons (in inches)

| Fathers | Sons | Fathers | Sons | Fathers | Sons | Fathers | Sons |
|---|---|---|---|---|---|---|---|
| 65.4 | 67.0 | 66.1 | 67.7 | 72.7 | 75.2 | 64.9 | 66.5 |
| 73.6 | 70.8 | 71.2 | 71.6 | 64.5 | 65.9 | 62.7 | 64.4 |
| 68.0 | 69.8 | 68.7 | 71.7 | 69.3 | 67.2 | 66.0 | 64.2 |
| 71.0 | 70.1 | 66.0 | 66.9 | 72.2 | 70.9 | 72.6 | 67.1 |
| 62.9 | 69.0 | 69.1 | 67.1 | 67.2 | 64.8 | 66.6 | 69.3 |
| 72.7 | 74.2 | 72.7 | 69.7 | 67.2 | 64.0 | 67.2 | 67.3 |
| 64.4 | 67.7 | 70.0 | 69.3 | 65.8 | 69.8 | 64.3 | 66.4 |
| 68.3 | 68.3 | 67.6 | 69.9 | 63.8 | 66.6 | 67.4 | 71.3 |
| 68.2 | 72.0 | 65.4 | 69.4 | 66.5 | 69.1 | 67.4 | 68.1 |
| 67.4 | 68.1 | 68.4 | 68.4 | 61.6 | 67.5 | 72.3 | 68.4 |
| 67.7 | 70.5 | 66.5 | 70.5 | 68.8 | 66.9 | 67.0 | 68.6 |
| 63.7 | 66.7 | 64.6 | 65.9 | 64.5 | 67.7 | 68.5 | 65.5 |
| 67.7 | 64.7 | 65.8 | 67.0 | 67.5 | 68.4 | 70.3 | 71.5 |
| 67.7 | 70.6 | 68.7 | 67.7 | 72.7 | 71.9 | 63.2 | 65.7 |
| 67.5 | 70.1 | 65.5 | 69.6 | 68.4 | 71.2 | 68.9 | 67.7 |
| 65.8 | 66.2 | 62.9 | 74.0 | 67.5 | 69.2 | 67.8 | 66.3 |
| 70.9 | 71.5 | 65.6 | 67.4 | 69.8 | 69.4 | 67.4 | 65.5 |
| 64.5 | 72.0 | 62.9 | 64.9 | 65.7 | 64.0 | 66.7 | 66.5 |
| 68.5 | 72.0 | 66.5 | 73.1 | 70.4 | 70.9 | 68.0 | 68.5 |
| 62.7 | 63.4 | 68.0 | 72.2 | 64.9 | 66.9 | 59.3 | 64.3 |
| 67.0 | 71.0 | 71.3 | 70.4 | 66.9 | 66.3 | 65.0 | 68.3 |
| 69.5 | 68.7 | 63.7 | 69.4 | 69.9 | 71.3 | 70.3 | 68.2 |
| 64.3 | 68.0 | 67.6 | 70.3 | 66.0 | 67.1 | 71.5 | 69.3 |
| 64.5 | 65.1 | 71.5 | 71.0 | 68.6 | 68.2 | 68.4 | 67.5 _(1,050)_ |
| 67.5 | 63.1 | 69.8 | 70.6 | 61.6 | 65.8 | 65.5 | 63.0 |
| 70.1 | 65.2 | 62.6 | 64.8 | 76.6 | 72.0 | 66.4 | 65.7 |
| 64.8 | 69.2 | 70.8 | 67.9 | 69.2 | 78.1 | 70.6 | 74.3 |
| 67.3 | 68.4 | 69.2 | 67.5 _(1,000)_ | 72.8 | 72.3 | 66.1 | 67.0 |
| 69.4 | 70.6 | 69.9 | 73.4 | 70.1 | 70.0 | 67.2 | 66.7 |
| 70.8 | 68.2 | 70.3 | 69.5 | 67.7 | 69.0 | 69.3 | 72.2 |
| 64.5 | 69.9 | 64.3 | 65.1 | 63.6 | 66.8 | 63.6 | 66.7 |
| 74.0 | 75.5 _(950)_ | 66.7 | 70.1 | 67.0 | 69.8 | 66.3 | 67.7 |
| 71.0 | 68.7 | 66.3 | 67.9 | 68.0 | 73.5 | 65.7 | 70.0 |
| 66.0 | 65.4 | 64.9 | 69.9 | 65.0 | 67.7 | 67.6 | 67.5 |
| 71.4 | 68.5 | 67.3 | 68.2 | 65.6 | 64.6 | 68.8 | 66.5 |
| 66.4 | 66.6 _(900)_ | 69.3 | 69.0 | 68.5 | 65.9 | 67.3 | 68.8 |
| 62.8 | 68.2 | 70.9 | 70.8 | 70.5 | 73.2 | 71.7 | 68.7 |
| 63.7 | 63.5 | 62.8 | 68.2 | 68.0 | 74.0 | 67.1 | 68.0 |
| 68.9 | 69.9 | 69.3 | 68.2 | 67.9 | 68.0 |  |  |
| 67.5 | 70.0 | 69.4 | 73.5 | 71.1 | 72.8 |  |  |
| 69.5 | 69.4 | 69.6 | 67.3 | 65.5 | 69.4 |  |  |
| 65.7 | 71.3 | 65.7 | 68.0 | 64.8 | 66.5 |  |  |
| 65.6 | 70.8 | 63.1 | 63.9 | 61.6 | 63.4 |  |  |
| 64.0 | 70.8 | 61.8 | 67.0 | 65.7 | 68.5 |  |  |
| 68.2 | 63.2 | 68.9 | 70.8 | 71.6 | 74.3 |  |  |
| 70.4 | 71.5 | 65.1 | 68.4 | 68.7 | 67.7 |  |  |
| 63.5 | 69.7 | 67.0 | 68.5 | 71.2 | 76.5 |  |  |
| 66.9 | 67.3 | 64.4 | 68.0 | 70.5 | 69.5 |  |  |
| 67.4 | 68.2 | 70.1 | 72.8 | 70.5 | 73.6 |  |  |
| 70.4 | 70.4 | 70.2 | 66.1 | 73.2 | 69.6 |  |  |
| 67.7 | 70.0 | 66.0 | 70.1 | 69.0 | 71.7 |  |  |
| 61.5 | 68.0 | 69.8 | 70.4 | 68.5 | 69.4 |  |  |
| 68.0 | 65.9 | 66.1 | 68.7 | 69.4 | 69.3 |  |  |
| 69.3 | 71.0 | 69.3 | 69.1 | 68.3 | 67.5 |  |  |

**1,064 TOTAL fathers and sons listed**

# Appendix B — Pearson and Lee's Data

## Fathers Sorted by Height (in inches)

| | | | | | | | | | | | | | | | | |
|---|---|---|---|---|---|---|---|---|---|---|---|---|---|---|---|---|
| 59.0 | 63.5 | 64.5 | 65.1 | 65.7 | 66.2 | 66.7 | 67.2 | 67.6 | 68.0 | 68.5 | 68.8 | 69.3 | 69.8 | 70.4 | 71.0 | 72.2 |
| 59.3 | 63.5 | 64.5 | 65.1 | 65.7 | 66.2 | 66.7 | 67.2 | 67.6 | 68.0 | 68.5 | 68.9 | 69.3 | 69.8 | 70.4 | 71.0 | 72.2 |
| 59.5 | 63.5 | 64.5 | 65.1 | 65.7 | 66.2 | 66.7 | 67.2 | 67.6 | 68.0 | 68.5 | 68.9 | 69.4 | 69.8 | 70.4 | 71.0 | 72.2 |
| 59.6 | 63.5 | 64.5 | 65.1 | 65.7 | 66.2 | 66.7 | 67.2 | 67.6 | 68.0 | 68.5 | 68.9 | 69.4 | 69.8 | 70.4 | 71.0 | 72.2 |
| 60.1 | 63.5 | 64.5 | 65.1 | 65.7 | 66.2 | 66.7 | 67.2 | 67.6 | 68.0 | 68.5 | 68.9 | 69.4 | 69.8 | 70.4 | [950] 71.0 | 72.2 |
| 60.1 | 63.5 | 64.5 | 65.2 | 65.7 | 66.2 | 66.7 | 67.2 | 67.6 | 68.0 | 68.5 | 68.9 | 69.4 | 69.9 | 70.4 | 71.0 | 72.2 |
| 60.5 | 63.5 | 64.5 | 65.2 | 65.7 | 66.2 | 66.7 | 67.2 | 67.7 | 68.0 | 68.5 | [700] 68.9 | 69.4 | 69.9 | 70.4 | 71.0 | 72.3 |
| 60.8 | 63.5 | 64.5 | 65.2 | 65.7 | 66.3 | 66.7 | 67.3 | 67.7 | 68.1 | 68.5 | 69.0 | 69.4 | 69.9 | 70.4 | 71.0 | 72.3 |
| 60.9 | 63.5 | 64.5 | 65.3 | 65.7 | 66.3 | 66.7 | [450] 67.3 | 67.7 | 68.1 | 68.5 | 69.0 | 69.4 | 69.9 | 70.4 | 71.1 | 72.3 |
| 61.0 | 63.5 | 64.5 | 65.3 | 65.8 | 66.3 | 66.7 | 67.3 | 67.7 | 68.1 | 68.5 | 69.0 | 69.4 | 69.9 | 70.5 | 71.1 | 72.4 |
| 61.0 | 63.5 | 64.5 | [200] 65.3 | 65.8 | 66.3 | 66.7 | 67.3 | 67.7 | 68.1 | 68.5 | 69.0 | 69.4 | 69.9 | 70.5 | 71.1 | 72.4 |
| 61.1 | 63.6 | 64.5 | 65.3 | 65.8 | 66.3 | 66.8 | 67.3 | 67.7 | 68.1 | 68.5 | 69.0 | 69.5 | 69.9 | 70.5 | 71.1 | 72.5 |
| 61.2 | 63.6 | 64.6 | 65.3 | 65.8 | 66.3 | 66.8 | 67.3 | 67.7 | 68.1 | 68.5 | 69.0 | 69.5 | 70.0 | 70.5 | 71.2 | 72.5 |
| 61.2 | 63.6 | 64.6 | 65.3 | 65.8 | 66.3 | 66.8 | 67.3 | 67.7 | 68.1 | 68.5 | 69.0 | 69.5 | 70.0 | 70.5 | 71.2 | 72.5 |
| 61.4 | 63.6 | 64.6 | 65.3 | 65.8 | 66.3 | 66.8 | 67.3 | 67.7 | 68.1 | 68.5 | 69.1 | 69.5 | 70.0 | 70.5 | 71.2 | 72.5 |
| 61.4 | 63.7 | 64.6 | 65.3 | 65.8 | 66.3 | 66.8 | 67.3 | 67.7 | 68.1 | 68.5 | 69.1 | 69.5 | 70.0 | 70.5 | 71.2 | 72.5 |
| 61.5 | 63.7 | 64.7 | 65.3 | 65.8 | 66.4 | 66.8 | 67.3 | 67.7 | 68.1 | 68.5 | 69.1 | 69.5 | 70.0 | [900] 70.5 | 71.2 | 72.5 |
| 61.5 | 63.7 | 64.7 | 65.3 | 65.8 | 66.4 | 66.8 | 67.3 | 67.7 | 68.1 | [650] 68.5 | 69.1 | 69.5 | 70.0 | 70.6 | 71.3 | 72.6 |
| 61.6 | 63.7 | 64.7 | 65.3 | 65.8 | 66.4 | 66.8 | 67.3 | 67.7 | 68.2 | 68.6 | 69.1 | 69.5 | 70.0 | 70.6 | 71.3 | 72.7 |
| 61.6 | 63.7 | 64.7 | 65.3 | 65.8 | 66.4 | [400] 66.8 | 67.3 | 67.7 | 68.2 | 68.6 | 69.1 | 69.5 | 70.0 | 70.6 | 71.3 | 72.7 |
| 61.6 | 63.7 | 64.7 | 65.4 | 65.8 | 66.4 | 66.8 | 67.3 | 67.8 | 68.2 | 68.6 | 69.1 | 69.5 | 70.0 | 70.6 | 71.4 | 72.7 |
| 61.6 | 63.7 | 64.7 | 65.4 | 65.8 | 66.4 | 66.8 | 67.3 | 67.8 | 68.2 | 68.6 | 69.1 | 69.5 | 70.0 | 70.6 | 71.4 | 72.7 |
| 61.6 | 63.7 | [150] 64.7 | 65.4 | 65.8 | 66.4 | 66.9 | 67.4 | 67.8 | 68.2 | 68.6 | 69.1 | 69.5 | 70.0 | 70.6 | 71.4 | 72.7 |
| 61.7 | 63.7 | 64.7 | 65.4 | 65.8 | 66.4 | 66.9 | 67.4 | 67.8 | 68.2 | 68.6 | 69.1 | 69.5 | 70.0 | 70.6 | 71.4 | 72.7 |
| 61.8 | 63.7 | 64.7 | 65.4 | 65.8 | 66.4 | 66.9 | 67.4 | 67.8 | 68.2 | 68.6 | 69.1 | 69.5 | 70.0 | 70.6 | 71.4 | 72.7 |
| 61.8 | 63.8 | 64.7 | 65.4 | 65.9 | 66.4 | 66.9 | 67.4 | 67.8 | 68.2 | 68.6 | 69.1 | 69.5 | 70.0 | 70.6 | 71.4 | 72.8 |
| 61.8 | 63.8 | 64.7 | 65.4 | 65.9 | 66.4 | 66.9 | 67.4 | 67.9 | 68.2 | 68.6 | 69.1 | 69.5 | 70.0 | 70.6 | 71.5 | 72.8 |
| 61.8 | 63.8 | 64.8 | 65.4 | 65.9 | 66.4 | 66.9 | 67.4 | 67.9 | 68.2 | 68.6 | 69.2 | 69.5 | 70.0 | 70.6 | 71.5 | 72.8 |
| 62.3 | 63.8 | 64.8 | 65.4 | 65.9 | 66.5 | 66.9 | 67.4 | 67.9 | 68.2 | 68.6 | 69.2 | 69.5 | 70.0 | [850] 70.6 | 71.5 | 72.9 |
| 62.4 | 63.9 | 64.8 | 65.5 | 65.9 | 66.5 | 67.0 | 67.4 | 67.9 | 68.2 | 68.6 | 69.2 | 69.5 | 70.0 | 70.6 | 71.5 | 72.9 |
| 62.4 | 63.9 | 64.8 | 65.5 | 65.9 | 66.5 | 67.0 | 67.4 | 67.9 | 68.2 | 68.6 | 69.2 | 69.5 | 70.0 | 70.6 | 71.5 | 72.9 |
| 62.4 | 63.9 | 64.8 | 65.5 | 65.9 | 66.5 | 67.0 | 67.4 | 67.9 | [600] 68.3 | 68.7 | 69.2 | 69.5 | 70.0 | 70.6 | 71.5 | 73.0 |
| 62.5 | 63.9 | 64.8 | 65.5 | 65.9 | 66.5 | 67.0 | 67.4 | 67.9 | 68.3 | 68.7 | 69.2 | 69.5 | 70.0 | 70.6 | 71.5 | 73.0 |
| 62.6 | 63.9 | 64.8 | 65.5 | 65.9 | 66.5 | 67.0 | 67.4 | 67.9 | 68.3 | 68.7 | 69.2 | 69.5 | 70.0 | 70.6 | 71.5 | 73.0 |
| 62.6 | 63.9 | 64.8 | 65.5 | 65.9 | [350] 66.5 | 67.0 | 67.5 | 67.9 | 68.3 | 68.7 | 69.2 | 69.5 | 70.1 | 70.7 | 71.6 | 73.1 |
| 62.6 | 64.0 | 64.8 | 65.5 | 66.0 | 66.6 | 67.0 | 67.5 | 67.9 | 68.3 | 68.7 | 69.2 | 69.6 | 70.1 | 70.7 | 71.6 | 73.2 |
| 62.6 | [100] 64.0 | 64.8 | 65.5 | 66.0 | 66.6 | 67.0 | 67.5 | 67.9 | 68.4 | 68.7 | 69.2 | 69.6 | 70.1 | 70.7 | 71.6 | 73.3 |
| 62.7 | 64.0 | 64.8 | 65.5 | 66.0 | 66.6 | 67.0 | 67.5 | 68.0 | 68.4 | 68.7 | 69.2 | 69.6 | 70.1 | 70.7 | 71.6 | 73.3 |
| 62.7 | 64.0 | 64.9 | 65.5 | 66.0 | 66.6 | 67.0 | 67.5 | 68.0 | 68.4 | 68.7 | 69.2 | 69.6 | 70.1 | 70.7 | 71.6 | 73.4 |
| 62.7 | 64.0 | 64.9 | 65.5 | 66.0 | 66.6 | 67.0 | 67.5 | 68.0 | 68.3 | 68.7 | 69.2 | [800] 69.6 | 70.1 | 70.7 | 71.6 | [1,050] 73.5 |
| 62.7 | 64.0 | 64.9 | 65.5 | 66.0 | 66.6 | 67.0 | 67.5 | 68.0 | 68.3 | 68.7 | 69.2 | 69.7 | 70.1 | 70.8 | 71.7 | 73.5 |
| 62.8 | 64.0 | 64.9 | 65.6 | 66.0 | 66.6 | 67.1 | 67.5 | 68.0 | 68.3 | 68.7 | 69.2 | 69.7 | 70.2 | 70.8 | 71.7 | 73.6 |
| 62.8 | 64.1 | 64.9 | 65.6 | 66.0 | 66.6 | 67.1 | 67.5 | 68.0 | 68.3 | 68.7 | [550] 69.2 | 69.7 | 70.2 | 70.8 | 71.7 | 74.0 |
| 62.9 | 64.1 | 64.9 | 65.6 | 66.0 | 66.6 | 67.1 | 67.5 | 67.9 | 68.4 | 68.7 | 69.2 | 69.7 | 70.2 | 70.8 | 71.8 | 74.4 |
| 62.9 | 64.2 | 65.0 | 65.6 | 66.0 | 66.6 | 67.1 | 67.5 | 67.9 | 68.4 | 68.7 | 69.3 | 69.6 | 70.2 | 70.8 | 71.8 | 74.5 |
| 62.9 | 64.3 | 65.0 | [300] 66.0 | 66.5 | 67.0 | 67.4 | 67.9 | 68.4 | 68.7 | 69.3 | 69.6 | 70.2 | 70.8 | 71.8 | 74.5 | |
| 63.0 | 64.3 | 65.0 | 65.6 | 66.6 | 67.0 | 67.5 | 67.9 | 68.4 | 68.7 | 69.3 | 69.6 | 70.2 | 70.8 | 71.8 | 74.6 | |
| [50] 63.0 | 64.3 | 65.0 | 65.6 | 66.1 | 66.6 | 67.0 | 67.5 | 68.0 | 68.4 | [1,000] 68.7 | 69.3 | 69.6 | 70.3 | 70.8 | 71.9 | 74.6 |
| 63.0 | 64.3 | 65.0 | 65.6 | 66.1 | 66.6 | 67.0 | 67.5 | 68.0 | 68.4 | 68.7 | 69.3 | 69.7 | 70.3 | 70.8 | 72.0 | 75.1 |
| 63.1 | 64.3 | 65.0 | 65.6 | 66.1 | 66.6 | 67.1 | 67.5 | 68.0 | 68.4 | 68.7 | 69.3 | 69.7 | 70.3 | 70.8 | 72.0 | 75.2 |
| 63.1 | 64.3 | 65.0 | 65.6 | 66.1 | 66.6 | 67.1 | 67.5 | 68.0 | 68.4 | 68.7 | 69.3 | 69.7 | 70.3 | 70.9 | 72.0 | 75.3 |
| 63.2 | 64.4 | 65.0 | 65.6 | 66.1 | 66.6 | 67.1 | 67.5 | 68.0 | 68.4 | 68.7 | 69.3 | 69.7 | 70.3 | 70.9 | 72.0 | 75.3 |
| 63.2 | 64.4 | 65.0 | 65.6 | 66.1 | 66.6 | 67.1 | 67.5 | 68.0 | 68.4 | 68.8 | 69.3 | 69.7 | 70.3 | 70.9 | [1,000] 72.0 | 76.6 |
| 63.2 | 64.4 | 65.0 | 65.6 | 66.1 | 66.6 | 67.1 | 67.5 | 68.0 | 68.4 | 68.8 | 69.3 | 69.7 | 70.3 | 70.9 | 72.0 | 76.6 |
| 63.3 | 64.4 | 65.0 | 65.6 | 66.1 | 66.6 | 67.1 | 67.5 | 68.0 | 68.4 | 68.8 | [750] 69.3 | 69.7 | 70.3 | 70.9 | 72.0 | |
| 63.3 | 64.4 | 65.0 | 65.6 | 66.1 | 66.6 | 67.1 | 67.5 | 68.0 | 68.4 | 68.8 | 69.3 | 69.7 | 70.3 | 70.9 | 72.0 | |
| 63.3 | 64.5 | 65.0 | 65.6 | 66.7 | 67.1 | 67.5 | 68.0 | 68.4 | 68.8 | 69.3 | 69.7 | 70.3 | 70.9 | 72.0 | | |
| 63.4 | 64.5 | 65.0 | 65.7 | 66.1 | 67.1 | [500] 67.5 | 68.0 | 68.4 | 68.8 | 69.3 | 69.8 | 70.3 | 70.9 | 72.0 | | |
| 63.4 | 64.5 | 65.1 | 65.7 | 66.2 | 66.7 | 67.1 | 67.5 | 68.0 | 68.4 | 68.8 | 69.3 | 69.8 | 70.3 | 70.9 | 72.0 | |
| 63.4 | 64.5 | [250] 65.1 | 65.7 | 66.2 | 66.7 | 67.1 | 67.5 | 68.0 | 68.5 | 68.8 | 69.3 | 69.8 | 70.3 | 70.9 | 72.1 | |
| 63.4 | 64.5 | 65.1 | 65.7 | 66.2 | 66.7 | 67.2 | 67.6 | 68.0 | 68.5 | 68.8 | 69.3 | 69.8 | 70.4 | 71.0 | 72.2 | |

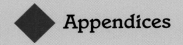

# Appendix C — Pearson and Lee's Data

## Sons Sorted by Height (in inches)

| | | | | | | | | | | | | | | | | |
|---|---|---|---|---|---|---|---|---|---|---|---|---|---|---|---|---|
| 59.7 | 64.5 | 65.5 | 66.3 | 66.8 | 67.3 | 67.7 | 68.0 | 68.4 | 68.8 | 69.3 | 69.7 | 70.2 | 70.8 | 71.3 | 72.0 | 73.4 |
| 59.9 | 64.5 | 65.5 | 66.3 | 66.8 | 67.3 | 67.7 | 68.0 | 68.4 | 68.9 | 69.3 | 69.7 | 70.2 | 70.8 | 71.3 | 72.0 | 73.5 |
| 60.9 | 64.5 | 65.5 | 66.3 | 66.8 | 67.3 | 67.7 | 68.0 | 68.4 | 68.9 | 69.3 | 69.7 | 70.2 | 70.8 | 71.3 | 72.1 | 73.5 |
| 61.4 | 64.5 | 65.5 | 66.3 | 66.9 | 67.3 | 67.7 | 68.0 | 68.4 | 68.9 | 69.3 | 69.7 | 70.2 | 70.8 | 71.3 | 72.1 | 73.5 |
| 62.0 | 64.6 | 65.5 | 66.4 | 66.9 | 67.3 | 67.7 | 68.0 | 68.4 | 68.9 | 69.3 | 69.8 | 70.2 | 70.8 | 71.3 | 72.1 | 73.5 |
| 62.3 | 64.6 | 65.5 | 66.4 | 66.9 | 67.3 | 67.7 | 68.0 | 68.4 | 68.9 | 69.3 | 69.8 | 70.3 | 70.8 | 71.3 | 72.1 | 73.5 |
| 62.4 | 64.6 | 65.5 | 66.4 | 66.9 | 67.3 | 67.7 | 68.0 | 68.4 | 68.9 | 69.3 | 69.8 | 70.3 | 70.8 | 71.3 | 72.2 | 73.6 |
| 62.5 | 64.6 | 65.6 | 66.4 | 66.9 | 67.3 | 67.7 | 68.0 | 68.4 | 68.9 | 69.3 | 69.8 | 70.3 | 70.8 | 71.4 | 72.2 | 73.6 |
| 62.5 | 64.6 | 65.6 | 66.4 | 66.9 | 67.3 | 67.7 | 68.1 | 68.4 | 68.9 | 69.3 | 69.8 | 70.3 | 70.8 | 71.4 | 72.2 | 73.6 |
| 62.5 | 64.6 | 65.6 | 66.4 | 66.9 | 67.3 | 67.7 | 68.1 | 68.5 | 68.9 | 69.3 | 69.8 | 70.3 | 70.8 | 71.4 | 72.2 | 73.6 |
| 62.7 | 64.7 | 65.6 | 66.4 | 66.9 | 67.3 | 67.7 | 68.1 | 68.5 | 69.0 | 69.3 | 69.8 | 70.3 | 70.8 | 71.4 | 72.2 | 73.6 |
| 62.8 | 64.7 | 65.6 | 66.4 | 66.9 | 67.3 | 67.7 | 68.1 | 68.5 | 69.0 | 69.3 | 69.8 | 70.3 | 70.8 | 71.4 | 72.2 | 73.6 |
| 62.8 | 64.7 | 65.6 | 66.5 | 66.9 | 67.4 | 67.7 | 68.1 | 68.5 | 69.0 | 69.4 | 69.8 | 70.3 | 70.8 | 71.4 | 72.2 | 73.6 |
| 62.9 | 64.7 | 65.6 | 66.5 | 66.9 | 67.4 | 67.7 | 68.1 | 68.5 | 69.0 | 69.4 | 69.8 | 70.3 | 70.9 | 71.4 | 72.3 | 73.6 |
| 62.9 | 64.7 | 65.7 | 66.5 | 66.9 | 67.4 | 67.7 | 68.1 | 68.5 | 69.0 | 69.4 | 69.8 | 70.3 | 70.9 | 71.4 | 72.3 | 73.8 |
| 63.0 | 64.8 | 65.7 | 66.5 | 66.9 | 67.4 | 67.7 | 68.1 | 68.5 | 69.0 | 69.4 | 69.8 | 70.3 | 70.9 | 71.4 | 72.3 | 73.9 |
| 63.1 | 64.8 | 65.7 | 66.5 | 66.9 | 67.4 | 67.7 | 68.1 | 68.5 | 69.0 | 69.4 | 69.8 | 70.4 | 70.9 | 71.4 | 72.3 | 73.9 |
| 63.1 | 64.8 | 65.7 | 66.5 | 67.0 | 67.4 | 67.7 | 68.1 | 68.5 | 69.0 | 69.4 | 69.9 | 70.4 | 70.9 | 71.4 | 72.3 | 74.0 |
| 63.1 | 64.8 | 65.7 | 66.5 | 67.0 | 67.4 | 67.7 | 68.1 | 68.5 | 69.0 | 69.4 | 69.9 | 70.4 | 70.9 | 71.5 | 72.3 | 74.0 |
| 63.2 | 64.8 | 65.7 | 66.5 | 67.0 | 67.4 | 67.7 | 68.1 | 68.5 | 69.0 | 69.4 | 69.9 | 70.4 | 70.9 | 71.5 | 72.3 | 74.0 |
| 63.4 | 64.8 | 65.7 | 66.5 | 67.0 | 67.4 | 67.7 | 68.1 | 68.5 | 69.0 | 69.4 | 69.9 | 70.4 | 70.9 | 71.5 | 72.4 | 74.0 |
| 63.4 | 64.9 | 65.7 | 66.5 | 67.0 | 67.4 | 67.8 | 68.1 | 68.5 | 69.0 | 69.4 | 69.9 | 70.4 | 70.9 | 71.5 | 72.4 | 74.0 |
| 63.4 | 64.9 | 65.7 | 66.5 | 67.0 | 67.4 | 67.8 | 68.2 | 68.5 | 69.0 | 69.4 | 69.9 | 70.4 | 70.9 | 71.5 | 72.4 | 74.0 |
| 63.4 | 64.9 | 65.8 | 66.5 | 67.0 | 67.4 | 67.8 | 68.2 | 68.5 | 69.0 | 69.4 | 69.9 | 70.4 | 70.9 | 71.5 | 72.4 | 74.2 |
| 63.4 | 64.9 | 65.8 | 66.5 | 67.0 | 67.5 | 67.8 | 68.2 | 68.5 | 69.0 | 69.4 | 69.9 | 70.4 | 70.9 | 71.5 | 72.5 | 74.2 |
| 63.5 | 64.9 | 65.8 | 66.5 | 67.0 | 67.5 | 67.8 | 68.2 | 68.5 | 69.0 | 69.4 | 69.9 | 70.4 | 71.0 | 71.5 | 72.5 | 74.2 |
| 63.5 | 64.9 | 65.8 | 66.6 | 67.0 | 67.5 | 67.8 | 68.2 | 68.6 | 69.1 | 69.4 | 69.9 | 70.4 | 71.0 | 71.5 | 72.5 | 74.2 |
| 63.5 | 64.9 | 65.8 | 66.6 | 67.0 | 67.5 | 67.8 | 68.2 | 68.6 | 69.1 | 69.4 | 69.9 | 70.4 | 71.0 | 71.6 | 72.5 | 74.3 |
| 63.5 | 64.9 | 65.8 | 66.6 | 67.0 | 67.5 | 67.8 | 68.2 | 68.6 | 69.1 | 69.4 | 69.9 | 70.4 | 71.0 | 71.6 | 72.6 | 74.3 |
| 63.6 | 64.9 | 65.8 | 66.6 | 67.0 | 67.5 | 67.8 | 68.2 | 68.6 | 69.1 | 69.5 | 70.0 | 70.4 | 71.0 | 71.6 | 72.6 | 74.3 |
| 63.6 | 65.0 | 65.8 | 66.6 | 67.0 | 67.5 | 67.8 | 68.2 | 68.6 | 69.1 | 69.5 | 70.0 | 70.4 | 71.0 | 71.6 | 72.6 | 74.3 |
| 63.7 | 65.0 | 65.9 | 66.6 | 67.0 | 67.5 | 67.8 | 68.2 | 68.6 | 69.1 | 69.5 | 70.0 | 70.4 | 71.0 | 71.6 | 72.7 | 74.3 |
| 63.8 | 65.0 | 65.9 | 66.6 | 67.0 | 67.5 | 67.8 | 68.2 | 68.6 | 69.1 | 69.5 | 70.0 | 70.5 | 71.0 | 71.7 | 72.7 | 74.4 |
| 63.8 | 65.0 | 65.9 | 66.6 | 67.0 | 67.5 | 67.9 | 68.2 | 68.6 | 69.2 | 69.5 | 70.0 | 70.5 | 71.0 | 71.7 | 72.7 | 74.5 |
| 63.8 | 65.0 | 65.9 | 66.6 | 67.0 | 67.5 | 67.9 | 68.2 | 68.6 | 69.2 | 69.5 | 70.0 | 70.5 | 71.0 | 71.7 | 72.7 | 74.5 |
| 63.9 | 65.0 | 65.9 | 66.6 | 67.0 | 67.5 | 67.9 | 68.2 | 68.6 | 69.2 | 69.5 | 70.0 | 70.5 | 71.0 | 71.7 | 72.7 | 74.7 |
| 63.9 | 65.0 | 65.9 | 66.6 | 67.1 | 67.5 | 67.9 | 68.2 | 68.6 | 69.2 | 69.5 | 70.0 | 70.5 | 71.0 | 71.7 | 72.7 | 74.8 |
| 63.9 | 65.0 | 66.0 | 66.6 | 67.1 | 67.5 | 67.9 | 68.2 | 68.6 | 69.2 | 69.5 | 70.0 | 70.5 | 71.0 | 71.7 | 72.8 | 74.9 |
| 63.9 | 65.0 | 66.0 | 66.6 | 67.1 | 67.5 | 67.9 | 68.2 | 68.6 | 69.2 | 69.5 | 70.0 | 70.5 | 71.1 | 71.7 | 72.8 | 75.1 |
| 63.9 | 65.0 | 66.0 | 66.6 | 67.1 | 67.5 | 67.9 | 68.3 | 68.7 | 69.2 | 69.5 | 70.0 | 70.5 | 71.1 | 71.7 | 72.8 | 75.2 |
| 63.9 | 65.1 | 66.0 | 66.6 | 67.1 | 67.5 | 67.9 | 68.3 | 68.7 | 69.2 | 69.5 | 70.0 | 70.5 | 71.1 | 71.7 | 72.8 | 75.2 |
| 64.0 | 65.1 | 66.0 | 66.6 | 67.1 | 67.5 | 67.9 | 68.3 | 68.7 | 69.2 | 69.5 | 70.0 | 70.5 | 71.1 | 71.8 | 72.8 | 75.4 |
| 64.0 | 65.1 | 66.0 | 66.7 | 67.1 | 67.5 | 68.0 | 68.3 | 68.7 | 69.2 | 69.5 | 70.0 | 70.5 | 71.1 | 71.8 | 72.9 | 75.5 |
| 64.0 | 65.1 | 66.0 | 66.7 | 67.1 | 67.6 | 68.0 | 68.3 | 68.7 | 69.2 | 69.5 | 70.0 | 70.5 | 71.1 | 71.8 | 73.0 | 75.5 |
| 64.1 | 65.1 | 66.0 | 66.7 | 67.1 | 67.6 | 68.0 | 68.3 | 68.7 | 69.2 | 69.6 | 70.0 | 70.5 | 71.1 | 71.8 | 73.0 | 75.7 |
| 64.2 | 65.2 | 66.1 | 66.7 | 67.1 | 67.6 | 68.0 | 68.3 | 68.7 | 69.2 | 69.6 | 70.0 | 70.5 | 71.1 | 71.8 | 73.0 | 76.4 |
| 64.2 | 65.2 | 66.1 | 66.7 | 67.1 | 67.6 | 68.0 | 68.3 | 68.7 | 69.2 | 69.6 | 70.0 | 70.5 | 71.1 | 71.8 | 73.1 | 76.5 |
| 64.2 | 65.2 | 66.1 | 66.7 | 67.1 | 67.6 | 68.0 | 68.3 | 68.7 | 69.2 | 69.6 | 70.0 | 70.6 | 71.2 | 71.8 | 73.1 | 76.5 |
| 64.3 | 65.3 | 66.1 | 66.7 | 67.1 | 67.6 | 68.0 | 68.3 | 68.7 | 69.2 | 69.6 | 70.0 | 70.6 | 71.2 | 71.8 | 73.1 | 76.6 |
| 64.3 | 65.3 | 66.1 | 66.7 | 67.2 | 67.6 | 68.0 | 68.3 | 68.7 | 69.2 | 69.6 | 70.1 | 70.6 | 71.2 | 71.8 | 73.2 | 77.4 |
| 64.3 | 65.3 | 66.2 | 66.7 | 67.2 | 67.6 | 68.0 | 68.3 | 68.7 | 69.2 | 69.6 | 70.1 | 70.6 | 71.2 | 71.8 | 73.2 | 77.4 |
| 64.3 | 65.3 | 66.2 | 66.7 | 67.2 | 67.6 | 68.0 | 68.3 | 68.8 | 69.2 | 69.6 | 70.1 | 70.6 | 71.2 | 71.8 | 73.2 | 77.5 |
| 64.3 | 65.3 | 66.2 | 66.7 | 67.2 | 67.6 | 68.0 | 68.3 | 68.8 | 69.2 | 69.7 | 70.1 | 70.6 | 71.2 | 71.9 | 73.3 | 78.0 |
| 64.4 | 65.3 | 66.3 | 66.7 | 67.2 | 67.7 | 68.0 | 68.3 | 68.8 | 69.3 | 69.7 | 70.1 | 70.6 | 71.3 | 71.9 | 73.3 | 78.1 |
| 64.4 | 65.3 | 66.3 | 66.8 | 67.2 | 67.7 | 68.0 | 68.3 | 68.8 | 69.3 | 69.7 | 70.1 | 70.7 | 71.3 | 72.0 | 73.3 | 78.6 |
| 64.4 | 65.4 | 66.3 | 66.8 | 67.2 | 67.7 | 68.0 | 68.3 | 68.8 | 69.3 | 69.7 | 70.1 | 70.7 | 71.3 | 72.0 | 73.3 | |
| 64.4 | 65.4 | 66.3 | 66.8 | 67.2 | 67.7 | 68.0 | 68.4 | 68.8 | 69.3 | 69.7 | 70.2 | 70.7 | 71.3 | 72.0 | 73.4 | |
| 64.4 | 65.4 | 66.3 | 66.8 | 67.2 | 67.7 | 68.0 | 68.4 | 68.8 | 69.3 | 69.7 | 70.2 | 70.7 | 71.3 | 72.0 | 73.4 | |
| 64.4 | 65.4 | 66.3 | 66.8 | 67.3 | 67.7 | 68.0 | 68.4 | 68.8 | 69.3 | 69.7 | 70.2 | 70.7 | 71.3 | 72.0 | 73.4 | |
| 64.4 | 65.4 | 66.3 | 66.8 | 67.3 | 67.7 | 68.0 | 68.4 | 68.8 | 69.3 | 69.7 | 70.2 | 70.7 | 71.3 | 72.0 | 73.4 | |
| 64.5 | 65.5 | 66.3 | 66.8 | 67.3 | 67.7 | 68.0 | 68.4 | 68.8 | 69.3 | 69.7 | 70.2 | 70.7 | 71.3 | 72.0 | 73.4 | |

(Running-count markers printed within the table: 50, 100, 150, 200, 250, 300, 350, 400, 450, 500, 550, 600, 650, 700, 750, 800, 850, 900, 950, 1,000, 1,050)

# Assessment

# Assessment Overview

Unit assessments in *Mathematics in Context* include two quizzes and a Unit Test. Quiz 1 is to be used anytime after students have completed Section B. Quiz 2 can be used after students have completed Section D. The Unit Test addresses most of the major goals of the unit. You can evaluate student responses to these assessments to determine what each student knows about the content goals addressed in this unit.

## Pacing

Each quiz is designed to take approximately 25 minutes to complete. The Unit Test is designed to be completed during a 45-minute class period. For more information on how to use these assessments, see the Planning Assessment section on the next page.

| Goals | Assessment Opportunities | Problem Levels |
|---|---|---|
| • Create and interpret a stem-and-leaf plot, histogram, or box plot from a single data set. | Quiz 1    Problem 1d<br>Quiz 2    Problems 2ab<br>Test        Problems 1bd, 2c, 3ab, 4ab<br>Statistics Project | |
| • Create and interpret a scatter plot. | Quiz 1    Problems 2abc | I |
| • Collect, organize, and interpret data in tabular form. | Quiz 1    Problems 1abc<br>Quiz 2    Problem 2a<br>Statistics Project | |
| • Find and interpret the mean, median, mode, or range of a data set. | Quiz 2    Problems 1abde<br>Test        Problems 1d, 2cf<br>Statistics Project | |
| • Understand the importance of a representative sample. | Quiz 1    Problems 1b, 2d<br>Quiz 2    Problem 1c<br>Test        Problem 4b | II |
| • Compare different representations. | Test        Problem 2e<br>Statistics Project | |
| • Understand the need to organize and summarize a large set of data. | Test        Problem 1a | |
| • Build an argument based on statistical measures and graphs. | Test        Problems 1d, 2d<br>Statistics Project | |
| • Develop a critical attitude toward using statistical methods. | Test        Problem 2g | III |
| • Solve problems by choosing appropriate statistical measures. | Quiz 2    Problem 1f<br>Test        Problems 1c, 2g<br>Statistics Project | |

## About the Mathematics

These assessment activities assess all of the goals for *Dealing with Data.* Refer to the Goals and Assessment Opportunities section on the previous page for information regarding the goals that are assessed in each problem. Some of the problems that involve multiple skills and processes address more than one unit goal. To assess students' ability to engage in non-routine problem solving (a Level III goal in the Assessment Pyramid), some problems such as the animal life spans problem on the Unit Test assess students' ability to use their skills and conceptual knowledge in different situations.

## Planning Assessment

These assessments are designed for individual assessment; however, some problems can be done in pairs or small groups. It is important that students work individually if you want to evaluate each student's understanding and abilities.

Make sure you allow enough time for students to complete the problems. If students need more than one class session to complete the problems, it is suggested that they finish during the next mathematics class, or you may assign select problems as a take-home activity. Students should be free to solve the problems their own way. Use of calculators on the quizzes or Unit Test is at the teacher's discretion.

If individual students have difficulties with any particular problems, you may give the student the option of making a second attempt after providing him or her a hint. You may also decide to use one of the optional problems or Extension activities not previously done in class as additional assessments for students who need additional help.

## Scoring

Solution and scoring guides are included for each quiz and the Unit Test. The method of scoring depends on the types of questions on each assessment. A holistic scoring approach is recommended for the Statistics Project and could also be used to evaluate an entire quiz.

Several problems require students to explain their reasoning or justify their answers. For these questions, the reasoning used by students in solving the problems as well as the correctness of the answers should be considered in your scoring and grading scheme.

Student progress toward goals of the unit should be considered when reviewing student work. Descriptive statements and specific feedback are often more informative to students than a total score or grade. You might choose to record descriptive statements of select aspects of student work as evidence of student progress toward specific goals of the unit that you have identified as essential.

*Use additional paper as needed.*

| Year | Time |
|------|------|
| 1896 | 12.00 |
| 1900 | 11.00 |
| 1904 | 11.00 |
| 1908 | 10.80 |
| 1912 | 10.80 |
| 1916 | ** |
| 1920 | 10.80 |
| 1924 | 10.60 |
| 1928 | 10.80 |
| 1932 | 10.30 |
| 1936 | 10.30 |
| 1940 | ** |
| 1944 | ** |
| 1948 | 10.30 |
| 1952 | 10.40 |
| 1956 | 10.50 |
| 1960 | 10.20 |
| 1964 | 10.00 |
| 1968 | 9.90 |
| 1972 | 10.14 |
| 1976 | 10.06 |
| 1980 | 10.25 |
| 1984 | 9.99 |
| 1988 | 9.92 |
| 1992 | 9.96 |
| 1996 | 9.84 |
| 2000 | 9.87 |
| 2004 | 9.85 |

1. The winning times for the Olympic men's 100-meter run are listed in the table. Overall, one could say that men are running faster and faster.

   a. Elaine took a sample of five consecutive times and concluded that men are NOT running faster. What sample do you think she picked? Why?

   b. Which sample of five consecutive times would you pick to show that men are indeed running faster?

   c. Between which two Olympics was the greatest progress in winning times? (In other words, when was the largest difference between two consecutive times?)

   d. What time would you predict for the next Olympics? Complete the graph below to support your answer.

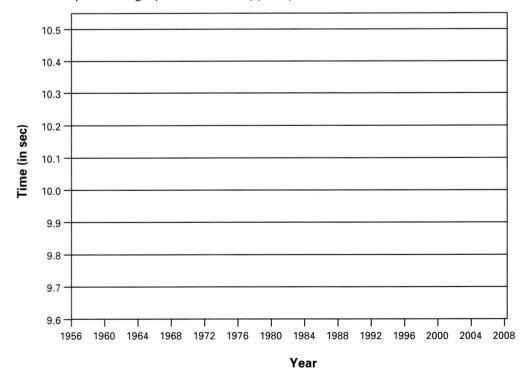

**2.** The table and scatter plot on this page show the approximate prices of some popular items in 1993 and in 2004. Note: The last five entries in the table have not been added to the scatter plot.

  **a.** Add the last five items in the table to the scatter plot.

  **b.** Describe or show where in the scatter plot you can find items where the price decreased over time.

  **c.** Do you agree or disagree with this statement: "In general, most items have increased in price since 1993."? Support your argument with information from the scatter plot.

  **d.** Do you think that the sample of items in the table is representative of what people typically spend their money on? Why or why not?

| Item | Price in 1993 ($) | Price in 2004 ($) |
|------|------|------|
| touchtone phone | 29.99 | 49.99 |
| woman's blouse | 45.00 | 65.00 |
| woman's fitness shoes | 59.99 | 69.99 |
| chocolate candy (0.5 lb) | 2.56 | 2.25 |
| radio-controlled vehicle | 49.99 | 69.99 |
| computer disks | 12.99 | 7.50 |
| French fries (regular) | 0.99 | 1.50 |
| scientific calculator | 19.99 | 14.00 |
| movie video | 19.95 | 9.95 |
| film (camera, 36 mm) | 6.57 | 5.95 |
| cotton pants (men's) | 24.00 | 24.00 |
| **piano/guitar lessons (0.5 hr)** | **16.00** | **20.00** |
| **jeans** | **55.00** | **65.00** |
| **ice cream sundae** | **3.00** | **4.50** |
| **movie tickets** | **6.00** | **9.00** |
| **board game** | **24.99** | **24.99** |

Price of Some Popular

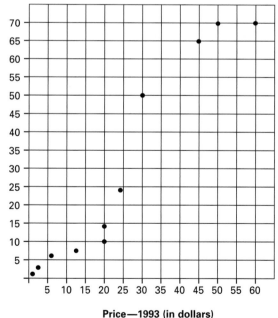

## Dealing with Data Quiz 2

*Use additional paper as needed.*

**1.** Given below are a sample from a very large set of data and a histogram that shows the complete set of shoe size data.

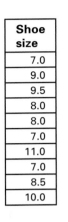

| Shoe size |
|-----------|
| 7.0 |
| 9.0 |
| 9.5 |
| 8.0 |
| 8.0 |
| 7.0 |
| 11.0 |
| 7.0 |
| 8.5 |
| 10.0 |

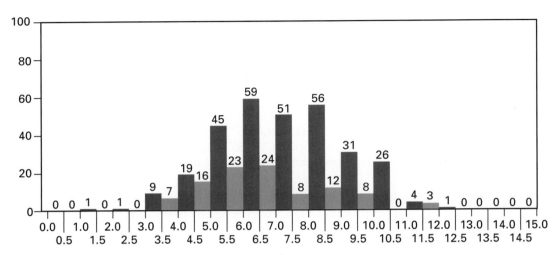

**a.** Find the mean shoe size for just the sample.

**b.** The mean of the complete data set is 7.0. Show how you could estimate this mean using the histogram. (Do not calculate the mean. Just show how to estimate it.)

**c.** Do you think the sample represents the large data set well? Why or why not?

**d.** Which shoe size is found most often in the large data set?

**e.** What is the mathematical name for this number?

**f.** Is the shoe size that is found most often a good way to describe the whole data set? Why or why not?

The heights (in centimeters) of 15 students are:

169, 164, 168, 192, 168, 170, 183, 173, 182, 176, 168, 172, 174, 165, 180

**2. a.** Using these data, create a stem-and-leaf plot for heights:

16 | .....
17 | ....

**b.** Draw one conclusion from the stem-and-leaf plot you made.

*Use additional paper as needed.*

1. Some animals live a very long time. Some have a very short life span. The table on this page contains the average life spans of several kinds of animals.

   **a.** How do you think these data were calculated? How would you do it?

   **b.** Study the data carefully. Write three statements about the data for the animals listed. On a separate piece of paper, make a graph to support what you wrote. Explain why you chose that particular type of graph.

   **c.** If you were asked to give a one-number summary of the average life span of the animals, what number would you choose and why?

   **d.** If the average life span of a human were added to the list, how would your graph and your one-number summary change?

| Animal | Average Life Span (years) |
|---|---|
| Asiatic Elephant | 40 |
| Beaver | 5 |
| Bison | 15 |
| Cat | 12 |
| Chipmunk | 6 |
| Cow | 15 |
| Deer | 8 |
| Dog | 12 |
| Elk | 15 |
| Giraffe | 10 |
| Gray Squirrel | 10 |
| Grizzly Bear | 25 |
| Guinea Pig | 4 |
| Horse | 20 |
| Kangaroo | 7 |
| Lion | 15 |
| Mouse | 3 |
| Opossum (American) | 1 |
| Pig (domestic) | 10 |
| Rabbit (domestic) | 5 |
| Red Fox | 7 |
| Sheep (domestic) | 12 |
| Wolf (maned) | 5 |
| Zebra (Grant's) | 15 |

**MEMORY**

2. The following words are one-syllable words that are easy to remember:

top, car, fix, leg, dot

Imagine that someone read a list of 20 words like these to you and then asked you to recall all the words.

  **a.** How many of the 20 words do you think you could remember (in any order)?

  **b.** Do you think that your memory gets better as you get older?

A psychologist (someone who studies how the mind works) conducted this test with students ages 6, 8, 10, and 12.

Here are the number of words the students remembered, by age group.

| Age 6 | 2, 2, 2, 2, 2, 3, 3, 3, 3, 3, 3, 4, 4, 4, 4, 4, 4, 5, 5, 6, 7 |
|-------|--------------------------------------------------------------|
| **Age 8** | 2, 3, 3, 3, 4, 4, 4, 4, 4, 5, 5, 5, 5, 5, 6 |
| **Age 10** | 3, 3, 3, 4, 4, 4, 4, 4, 4, 5, 5, 5, 5, 5, 5, 5, 5, 5, 5, 6, 7 |
| **Age 12** | 4, 4, 4, 5, 5, 5, 5, 5, 6, 6, 6, 6, 6, 6, 6, 8 |

  **c.** What are the mode and median for each age group?

| Age | Mode | Median |
|-----|------|--------|
| 6 | | |
| 8 | | |
| 10 | | |
| 12 | | |

  **d.** Study the data. What relationship do you see between age and memory? Justify your argument with specific numbers from the data.

*Use additional paper as needed.*

To display and analyze the data to find out what relationship exists between age and memory, Eileen proposes to use histograms. Fidel prefers using box plots.

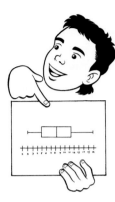

**e.** What type of graph do you think is best to study the relationship between age and memory? Give reasons for your choice.

**f.** Calculate the mean for each group. What do these numbers tell you?

Age 6:

Age 8:

Age 10:

Age 12:

**g.** Would you choose the mean, the mode, or the median to describe the typical number of words people in each age group can remember? Explain your choice.

**3.** The box plot below show the heights of women and men. There are 195 women and 209 men in this sample.

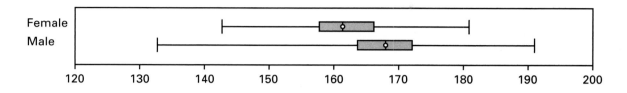

**Height — Women and Men**

**a.** Which gender has a greater range in height, female or male?

**b.** Daniel says, "Almost all men are taller than the shortest women." Do you agree with him? Why or why not?

**4.** The box plot below shows the heights of left-handed women and men and right-handed women and men. There are 22 left-handed women, 173 right-handed women, 29 left-handed men and 180 right-handed men in this sample.

**Height**

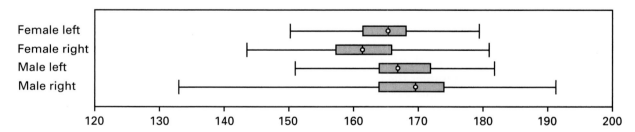

**a.** What percent of left-handed women are taller than the median of the right-handed women?

**b.** From this box-plot, could one conclude that left-handed women are taller than right-handed women and that right-handed men are taller than left-handed men? Why or why not?

# Dealing with Data Quiz 1
## Solution and Scoring Guide

| Possible student answer | Suggested number of score points | Problem level |
|---|---|---|
| **1. a.** Possible set of five Olympic Games: 1932 – 1936 – 1948 – 1952 – 1956 (though the war years 1940 and 1944 did not give any data). Accept any answer that shows a sample of consecutive years that does not show a decrease in time. | 1 | I |
| **b.** Possible set of five Olympic Games: 1980 – 1984 – 1988 – 1992 – 1996. Accept any answer that shows a sample of consecutive years that shows a decrease in time. | 1 | I/II |
| **c.** 1896 – 1900 (a difference of one second) | 2 | I |
| **d.** Sample prediction, using a graph: | 2 (for a reasonable prediction close to 9.8) | I |

I predict a time close to 9.85 for the next Olympics. The last three Olympics the time was very close to 9.85, and it does not seem to change very much.

Or: There is a natural limit to the time that can be reached over 100 m. I do not expect the time to change very much any more after looking at the last 12 years.

(for a reasonable explanation)

1

| Possible student answer | Suggested number of score points | Problem level |
|---|---|---|
| **2. a.** Sample graph.  | 3 | I |
| **b.** Students may say "the bottom right half of the scatter plot," mark points in this region, or sketch a diagonal where the 1993 prices are equal to the 2004 prices. The items for which prices decreased over time are below the dotted line. | 2 | I |
| **c.** Sample statement: "I do agree with the statement because most data are above the dotted line in my graph." | 2 | I |
| **d.** Sample student reasoning: I do not think this sample is representative because most of the time people spend money on food. Accept any reasonable answer. | 1 | II |
| **Total score points** | 15 | |

Sample graph:

**Price of Some Popular**

Current Price—2004 (in dollars) vs Price—1993 (in dollars)

**Dealing with Data Quiz 2**
**Solution and Scoring Guide**

| Possible student answer | Suggested number of score points | Problem level |
|---|---|---|
| **1. a.** The mean shoe size for the sample is 8.5.<br><br>$(7.0 + 9.0 + 9.5 + 8.0 + 8.0 + 7.0 + 11.0 + 7.0 + 8.5 + 10.0 = 85; \ 85 \div 10 = 8.5)$ | 2 | I |
| **b.** Students should describe a reasonable approach to estimating the mean.<br><br>Sample student answer: You can use a compensation strategy looking at the heights of the bars. | 1 | I |
| **c.** The sample does not represent the whole data set well because of the great deviation from the estimated mean of the whole data set. Accept any comparable reasoning. | 1 | II |
| **d.** The shoe size found most often is 6.0. | 1 | I |
| **e.** This number is called the *mode*. | 1 | I |
| **f.** Sample student answer: The mode of the whole data set is 6.0. But 7.0 and 8.0 are rather close to that number, so the shoe size found most often (the mode) is not a good way to describe the data set. | 2 | III |
| **2. a.** 16 I 4 5 8 8 8 9<br><br>17 I 0 2 3 4 6<br><br>18 I 0 2 3<br><br>19 I 2 | 2 | I |
| **b.** Possible responses may include finding the mean, mode, or median, or describing a context related result (such as, "All students are less than 2 m tall."). | 2 | I |
| **Total score points** | 12 | |

| Possible student answer | Suggested number of score points | Problem level |
|---|---|---|
| **1. a.** Possible student answer: Researchers may have tracked animals during their lifetime. Students may suggest that data from zoo animals can be used.<br><br>(Accept reasonable answers.) | 2 | III |
| **b.** Sample answers: (Note that students need to write three statements and create one graph.)<br><br>The shortest life span is that of an opossum, one year.<br><br>The range of life spans is from 1 to 40 years.<br><br>Most life spans seem to be under 20 years.<br><br>Five animals have a life span of 15 years.<br><br>The elephant lives far longer than the others, 40 years.<br><br>Sample graph for a stem-and-leaf plot, (A histogram or number line plot is also possible,)<br><br>0 | 1 3 4 5 5 5 6 7 7 8<br>1 | 0 0 0 2 2 2 5 5 5 5 5<br>2 | 0 5<br>3 |<br>4 | 0<br>key: 1 | 5 means 15 years. | 5<br>(1 score point for each correct statement, 2 score points for a correct graph) | I |
| **c.** The mean is 12 years, but it does not make sense in this context: there is a large influence by the outliers 27 and 40. The mode is 15 years but does not really represent the center of the data. The median would probably be the best choice, 10. | 2<br>(For a choice with a reasonable explanation) | III |
| **d.** Answers depend on the choice students made for problem 1c. The average life span of a human is about 75 years. This number would influence the mean, the mode would stay the same, and the median would change from 10 to 11. | 1 | I/III |

# Dealing with Data Unit Test
## Solution and Scoring Guide

| Possible student answer | Suggested number of score points | Problem level |
|---|---|---|
| **2. a.** Accept a reasonable answer. Students will probably not remember more than ten words. | 1 | I |
| **b.** Most students will answer that memory gets worse as you get very much older. Accept a reasonable answer. | 1 | I |
| **c.** | 8 | I |
| **d.** The data suggests that memory continues to improve as students grow older. Check student's numbers used to justify their answer. | 2 | III |
| **e.** Accept reasonable choices and explanations. Box plots are useful to compare different groups. Histograms show the original data. | 2 (For a choice with a reasonable explanation) | II |
| **f.** The mean for each age group is: • age 6: 3.6 • age 8: 4.1 • age 10: 4.6 • age 12: 5.4 | 4 | I |
| **g.** The mean or median makes most sense. The mode is not very useful since there are two modes at age 6 and at age 8. There are no outliers. The mean and median are close together. | 2 | III |

Table for **2. c.**:

| Age | Mode | Median |
|---|---|---|
| 6 | 3 and 4 | 3 |
| 8 | 4 and 5 | 4 |
| 10 | 5 | 5 |
| 12 | 6 | 5.5 |

| Possible student answer | Suggested number of score points | Problem level |
|---|---|---|
| **3. a.** male (no explanation required) | 1 | I |
| **b.** Sample student answer:<br><br>Yes, I agree. 25% of the women are taller than 1.66 m. 50% of the men are taller than 1.68 m | 2 | I |
| **4 a.** 75% of 22 women or 17 (or 16) women | 2 | I |
| **b.** No, that is not possible because the number of people is not comparable. You cannot generalize such a statement based on a relatively small number of people. | 1 | I/II |
| **Total score points** | 36 | |

Use an almanac from 2004 or later, or another recent source, to look up information about one or more of the topics listed below. Organize the data in a stem-and-leaf plot, a histogram, and a box plot. Be sure to:

*   calculate the mean, median, and mode;

*   include labels on your graphs for scales, proper intervals, and a title;

*   use graph paper or a computer;

*   do your work neatly;

*   write a summary about your data. Do you see a pattern, conclusion, or relationship in the data? Which graphical representation is the most accurate?

**Topics:**

1.  Age of presidents at their inauguration, Democrats vs. Republicans

2.  Annual inches of precipitation in the United States, northern states vs. southern states

3.  Earnings by occupation, male vs. female

4.  Miles per gallon for automobiles, imports vs. U.S. cars

5.  Scores in any of the college football bowl games since 1950, Pac 10 vs. Big 10

6.  Scores for the Super Bowls since 1967, AFC vs. NFC

7.  Batting average for the World Series for the last 20 years, American League vs. National League

8.  Years in which states were accepted into the United States, northern states vs. southern states

9.  Your choice (please consult with your teacher first)

## Materials

Students should be provided with at least three sheets of graph paper, a ruler, and a calculator. Students should also have access to an almanac or the Internet to find their data set.

## Objectives

Most of the major goals of this unit are assessed in this project. You may choose to adapt the assignment to address specific goals.

## Planning

You may want to use this assessment as a long-range project that students work on at home over a one-week period. You might decide to use this assessment as a small group activity to be completed and shared in class.

## Scoring Suggestions

An analytic or holistic scoring scheme can be used to grade this work. If you choose to use an analytic approach, a certain number of points would be assigned for completing each part of the project. For example, the correct calculation of the mean, median, and mode for each data set could be worth 10 points each. Creating stem-and-leaf plots, histograms, and box plots for each data set could be worth 30 points each. A complete written summary could be worth another 20 points. Bonus points could be awarded for including additional graphs, such as scatter plots.

For a holistic scoring approach, the following rubric could be used or adapted, depending or your expectations for students.

**4 pts**: Student work shows a complete understanding of the project. The summary includes a complete/acceptable solution and a fully-developed explanation that is clearly communicated. Graphs and descriptive statistics are neat and easy to follow.

**3 pts**: Student work shows an understanding of the project. The graphs and descriptive statistics are correct/acceptable but the written summary may contain minor errors or not be fully communicated. Graphs and descriptive statistics are easy to follow.

**2 pts**: Student work shows evidence of a reasonable approach to the project, but also indicates gaps in conceptual understanding. Some statistics may be incorrect, and the written summary may be incomplete, vague, or muddled.

**1 pts**: Student work shows evidence that the student has engaged in the project. The graphs and/or statistics contain major mathematical errors, and the written summary contains serious flaws in reasoning.

**0 pts**: The student either did not attempt to complete the project or gave incorrect/irrelevant graphs and statistics with no written explanation.

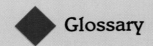 Glossary

# Glossary

The Glossary defines all vocabulary words marked in the Student Book. It includes the mathematical terms that may be new to students, as well as words having to do with the contexts introduced in the unit. (Note: The Student Book has no glossary. This is in order to allow students to construct their own definitions, based on their personal experiences with the unit activities.) The definitions below are specific to the use of the terms in this unit. The page numbers given are from this Teacher's Guide.

**box plot** (p. 38) a graphic way of showing a summary of data using the median, quartiles, and extremes of the data. A box plot makes it easy to see how the data are spread out and where they are concentrated; box plots are also known as box-and-whisker plots.

**coordinate system** (p. 7) a grid having intersecting horizontal and vertical number lines and in which a set of numbers is used to represent a point. The number line going across the grid in the left/right direction is called **horizontal axis.** The number line going up and down on a grid is called **vertical axis.** The fixed point of intersection of the horizontal and vertical axes is called **origin.**

**frequency table** (p. 15) a table in which the number of times each value (or category) occurs—its frequency—is listed

**histogram** (p. 18) a bar graph that shows a frequency distribution made up of rectangles whose widths represent class intervals and whose areas are proportional to the corresponding frequencies

**measures of central tendency** (p. 12B) one-number values used to summarize data, such as the mean, median, and mode

**mean** (p. 26) a number found by dividing the sum of a set of data by the number of items in the set

**median** (p. 36) the value in an ordered data set that is greater than one-half of the values and less than the other half

**mode** (p. 15) the value that occurs most often in a data set

**number line** (p. 39) a line representing the set of all real numbers; the numbers on a number line are placed at equal distances (as on a ruler)

**population** (p. 5) a large, complete group of data; a smaller **sample** (group taken from a larger population) is often taken in order to make inferences about a much larger population

**quartile** (p. 34A) medians of each half of a data set

**range** (p. 29) the difference between the highest and lowest data points

**scatter plot** (p. 8) a graph made by plotting points on a coordinate system

**stem-and-leaf plot** (p. 16) a frequency distribution made by arranging data so that all digits except the last digit are the stems. The last digits are leaves. Both stems and leaves are arranged in order from least to greatest.

**whiskers** (p. 38) the line segments at either end of the box in a box plot

# Blackline Masters

# ◆ Letter to the Family

## Dear Family,

Very soon your child will begin the *Mathematics in Context* unit *Dealing with Data.* The unit is about statistics and will begin to teach your child how to analyze data. Students will learn how to make graphs and to calculate different numbers to describe data. In the process they will answer questions such as:

- whether tall parents have tall children;
- how fast cheetahs run;
- how big students' hands are relative to others' hands; and
- how old presidents of the United States tend to be when inaugurated.

Look for data in newspapers and magazines and discuss how they might have been collected and why. If there is a graph in an article, is it appropriate, and is it essential to the article? Find a question in which your child is interested and help collect and analyze data that will answer the question. You might compare sports teams, investigate which television channels are the most popular, or analyze different supermarket prices. Your child will also collect some data from family members during the unit.

Have fun "dealing with data"!

### Dear Student,

How big is your hand? Do you think it is bigger than, smaller than, or the same size as most people's hands? How can you find out?

22 cm   24 cm   17 cm

How fast does a cheetah run? Do you think it runs much faster than, a little faster than, or at about the same speed as other animals? How can you find out?

Do tall people have tall children?

How can you find out?

In the *Mathematics in Context* unit *Dealing with Data,* you will examine questions like these and learn how to answer them. By collecting and examining data, you can answer questions that are interesting and often important.

While you are working through this unit, think of your own questions that you can answer by collecting and examining data. One of the best uses of mathematics is to help you answer questions you find interesting.

Sincerely,

*The Mathematics in Context Development Team*

Sincerely,

*The Mathematics in Context Development Team*

# Pearson and Lee Data

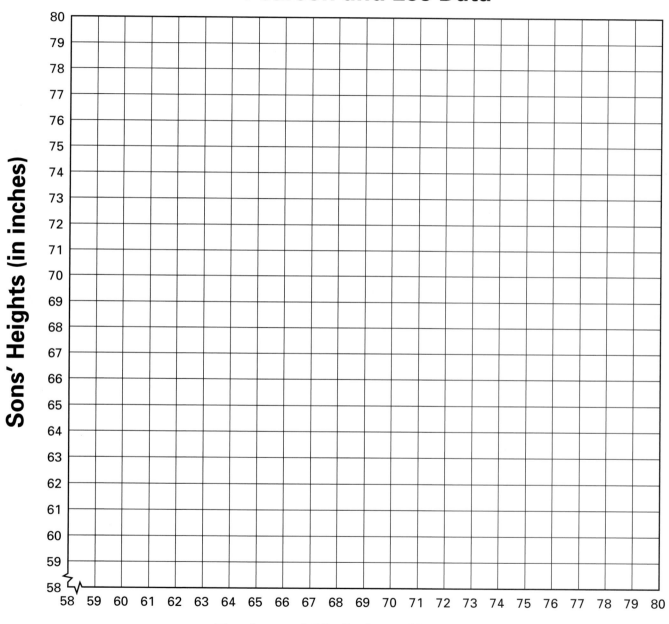

**Sons' Heights (in inches)**

**Fathers' Heights (in inches)**

Name _____

# Pearson and Lee Data

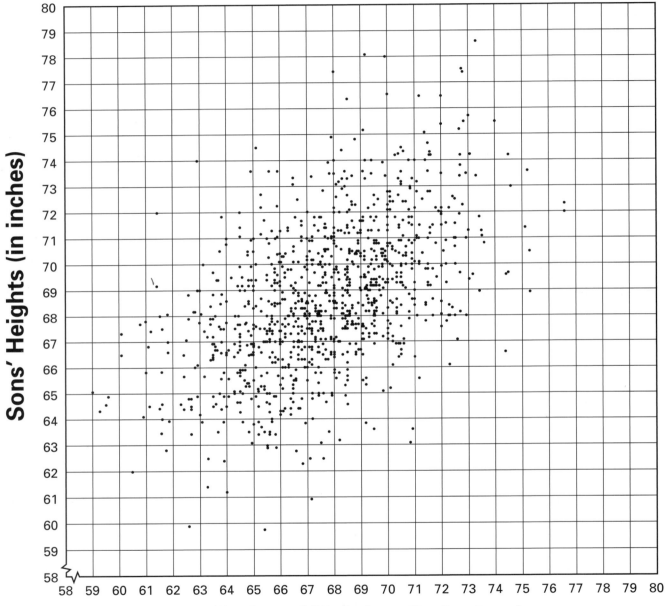

*x-axis:* Fathers' Heights (in inches)

*y-axis:* Sons' Heights (in inches)

Name _____

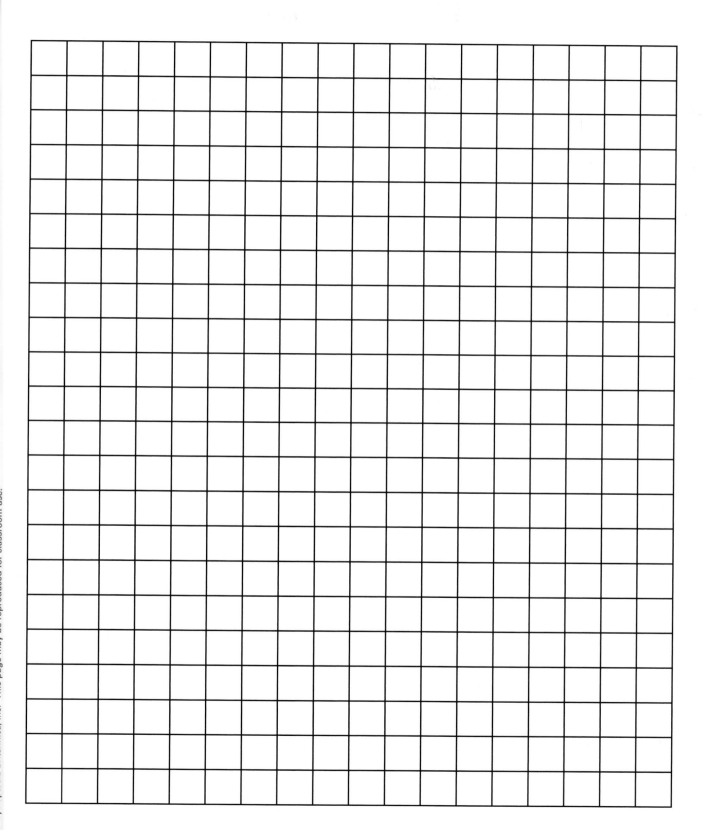

Name _____

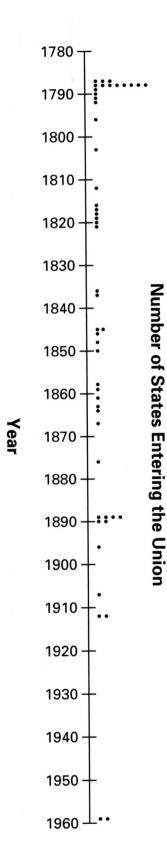